The Mystique of Dreams

G. William Domhoff

The Mystique of Dreams

A Search for Utopia
through Senoi Dream Theory

University of California Press

Berkeley   Los Angeles   London

University of California Press
Berkeley and Los Angeles, California
University of California Press, Ltd.
London, England
© 1985 by
The Regents of the University of California
Printed in the United States of America

1   2   3   4   5   6   7   8   9

Library of Congress Cataloging in Publication Data

Domhoff, G. William.
    The mystique of dreams.

    Bibliography: p.
    Includes index.
    1. Dreams.   2. Stewart, Kilton, 1902-   3. Utopias.   4. United
States–Civilization–1945-   5. Senoi (Malaysian people)–Psychology.
6. Senoi (Malaysian people)–Social life and customs.   I. Title.
BF1078.D58   1986   154.6'3   85–970
ISBN 0–520–05504–7

Contents

Preface

This book began with a casual trip to the campus library to find new information for a lecture to my introductory course on dreams. Students were asking about topics I hadn't given much thought to in many years, and I wanted to bring myself up to date. At that point I had no inkling of the complex and fascinating intellectual journey that was to unfold.

I punched into the computer under "Senoi," and up came one book, anthropologist Robert K. Dentan's 1968 monograph entitled *The Semai: A Nonviolent People of Malaya*. It came up, I quickly learned, because the Semai are a Senoi people.

I read Dentan's well-written and very sensitive account of his fourteen months living among the Semai with great interest, but it told me nothing about the unusual dream principles the Senoi are said to utilize. I then wrote to Professor Dentan, who sent me his yet-unpublished paper, "A Dream of Senoi," since published in the Special Studies Series of the Council on International Studies at the State University of New York at Buffalo.

Dentan's findings about Senoi dream theory whetted my appetite to learn more. We corresponded back and forth and even thought about writing a popular article on the topic that would draw on our separate trainings in anthropology and psychology. I also read the papers of several other anthropologists who had studied Senoi peoples and talked with the two who were most accessible to me, Clayton Robarchek of California State University, Chico, and Geoffrey Benjamin of the University of Singapore (a visitor to California in the summer of 1983).

Most of all, however, it was my correspondence with Dentan that led me into the further research that is the basis for this book. Never having met, we found it difficult to collaborate on a paper, but his original work on the Senoi remains a major basis for Chapter 2, and I am grateful for the help and encouragement he gave me.

After satisfying myself on the Senoi and their dream theory, I then turned to a detailed study of Kilton R. Stewart, an anthropologist and psychologist whose writings were the basis for the widespread interest in the theory. Here I was aided by several people who knew Stewart very well—his brother, Omer C. Stewart, himself a distinguished anthropologist emeritus at the University of Colorado; Sir Edmund R. Leach, one of the world's most eminent anthropologists, now retired from Cambridge University; Dorothy Nyswander, a retired psychologist, who was one of Stewart's undergraduate teachers as well as a lifelong friend; Margaret Nyswander Manson, who came to know Stewart through her sister Dorothy and rented a room to him in her home in New York City in the forties; Nancy Grasby, who was with Stewart as a stenographer and typist on his trip to the island of Botel Tobago off Formosa in late 1936; Claudia Parsons, who traveled with Stewart in 1937 and 1938; and Clara Stewart Flagg, who became his assistant in the early forties and later his wife.

I also benefited in my understanding of Stewart from briefer correspondence and conversations with anthropologist Francis L. K. Hsu, who knew Stewart in Peking in 1936; anthropologist Raymond Firth, who served as one of Stewart's dissertation examiners; and graphics designer Patricia A. Olson, who knew Stewart in New York in the sixties.

To understand how Senoi dream theory caught on in the United States, I talked with several people who were of great help: Charles Tart, a psychologist at the University of California, Davis; Joe Kamiya, a psychologist at the University of California, San Francisco; the late Tom Allen, a professor of art at Cabrillo College in Santa Cruz, California, and a fellow in the first Residence Program at Esalen Institute in 1966; George Leonard, a former vice-president of Esalen Institute and the author of *Education and Ecstasy*; Michael Murphy, the co-founder of Esalen Institute; Walter T. Anderson, the author of *The Upstart Spring*, a book on Esalen; and Edward Maupin, a clinical psychologist in San Diego who was active at Esalen Institute in the sixties.

My perspective on how Senoi dream theory fits into wider themes of the sixties was aided immeasurably by conversations with my colleague James T. Clifford, a professor of the history of consciousness at the University of California, Santa Cruz. Clifford also helped me greatly in formulating my general ideas on dream theories and how they relate to larger issues in scientific work and the sociology of ideas, problems that are addressed in the final chapter. The final chapter also benefited from the suggestions of Waud Kracke, an anthropologist at the University of Illinois, Chicago Circle, with a wide-ranging and cross-cultural perspective on dream research. The comments of three anonymous reviewers were also important in shaping the concluding chapter.

James Clifford, Robert Dentan, Francis Hsu, Sir Edmund Leach, George Leonard, Clayton Robarchek, Charles Tart, and Robert Van de Castle gave me extremely helpful substantive and editorial suggestions on all or parts of the manuscript. Michael Kimmel, a sociologist at Rutgers University, Cynthia R. Margolin, a psychologist at San Jose State University, and Deborah Wright, a graduate student in psychology at the University of California, Santa Cruz, provided excellent editorial suggestions that led to major changes and additions. I also am indebted to Beth W. Ghiloni, a graduate student in sociology at the University of California, Santa Cruz, for valuable organizational suggestions that made the argument flow more smoothly. Ghiloni also helped me to work out several of the ideas in the final chapter.

As this accounting should make clear, I am deeply grateful

to all these people for their invaluable help. It is literally true
in this instance that the book would not have been written
without their assistance, for it was out of my interactions
with them that the ideas for this book slowly emerged. Of
course, none of them is responsible for any errors or misin-
terpretations in the book. I am thankful for their openness as
well as for the social and scholarly courtesies that they af-
forded me.

Since I may be indentified by some readers as the author of
earlier books in political sociology, perhaps I should explain
that my original training was in psychology and that I did
my dissertation research on dreams with the help of Calvin
S. Hall and Joe Kamiya. The results of that work were published in the *Archives of General Psychiatry* in 1964 in three
articles co-authored with Kamiya. I also was the primary author of three other papers on dreams that appeared in the
sixties and the co-author of four papers with Hall. Then, too,
I taught seminars on dreams from 1966 to 1970, even though
my interest in political sociology was by then in ascendance,
and I resumed teaching dream courses in 1978.

In any event, this book is as much a study in the sociology
of ideas as it is a study of dreams. I doubt that I would have
started it if I had not studied dreams as a graduate student,
but I am sure I was able to finish it only because I had become
a sociologist in the meantime.

1

The New
Mystique of Dreams

Everywhere we turn, the strange and sometimes frightening picture stories of the night called dreams are seen as somehow significant, as somehow meaningful. In many cultures, and in times past, dreams have been treated with awe and regarded as a mystery. As we know from the Bible, dreams are often a source of prophecies. In other places, they have been seen as a key to the elusive secrets of life that people persist in believing must exist somewhere. Some sages even see dreams as a way out of those universal human feelings of restless dissatisfaction that lead theorists to create such grandiose explanatory concepts as original sin, repression, and alienation. There is, in short, a mystique about dreams, an attitude of mystical veneration, and a feeling that they can be comprehended only by those who have gone through an initiatory process into a cult of deeper understanding.

Historically, dreams are one reason for the belief in a soul that is separable from the body: some of our dream adventures seem so real that we feel they must have happened even though our bodies were asleep. Dreams also contribute to the notion that there is a life after death—deceased relatives and other loved ones sometimes reappear with such a stunning reality in our dreams, talking with us in animated fashion or showing great emotion, that it is hard to believe, even when we know better, that their presence is merely the product of our imaginations.

The mystique of dreams plays a formative role in the widespread human belief in mental telepathy or thought transference. In some surveys, as many as 60 to 70 percent of those who say they have experienced mental telepathy do so on the basis of a dream, usually a dream in which a friend or relative dies, becomes ill, or has an accident in the dream—only to have the dreamer awaken to find that this event actually has occurred or occurs shortly thereafter.[1]

The mystique of dreams is enhanced by the pivotal role dreams can play in times of transition, whether those transitions be cultural or personal. Dreams, for example, are often crucial in times of cultural crisis, when a society is facing attack or disintegration. At these moments, there will invariably arise new prophets or culture heroes, and their new preachings will be based on a dream or something closely related to a dream in popular thinking—a vision. For individuals, dreams are sometimes seen as critical turning points, particularly in the transition from youth to adulthood in tribal societies, where one's future calling may be decided on the basis of a dream, often a dream that is sought through physical isolation, fasting, drugs, or meditation. Or dreams may be very important when a person becomes ill, whether physically or psychologically. Shamans and other primitive healers often use dreams in a very dramatic way to diagnose illness or attempt a cure.

Western societies of the last century have tended to downgrade the importance of dreams, but even they are no exception to the claim that dreams everywhere and always have been seen as somehow significant and meaningful. What differentiates these societies from all others is the belief that dreams reveal the hidden aspects of our personalities, that their meaning can be found in the pattern of secret wishes and fears underlying the benign personas we try to present to the rest of the world.

The idea that dreams contain unconscious wishes and fears began in 1900 with the publication of Sigmund Freud's monumental *The Interpretation of Dreams*. By listening to his patients say whatever came into their heads about each part or element of their dreams, a process he called free association, Freud came to the conclusion that dreams were the "royal road to the unconscious." That striking metaphor has dominated educated commentary on dreams ever since, and a long series of rigorous quantitative studies by the psychologist Calvin Hall on dreams collected all over the world has tended to substantiate that metaphor.[2]

However, for all the interest in Freudian psychology and its many offshoots, dreams have not enjoyed a position of esteem for the great majority of educated Westerners. Dreams are most frequently viewed as bits and pieces of random nonsense tossed off by a brain that is working at half speed, or as untrained fingers running randomly on a piano keyboard, as Freud characterized the dominant view in 1917.[3] More recently, with the ascendance of the computer as the latest metaphor for mental functioning, dreams have been characterized as the processing of irrelevant information in order to clear the mind for the next day's work, as mere "glitches" in the computer programs that are analogized with our mental processors.[4] Thus, interest in the meaning of dreams has been confined to those social scientists who study neurotic personalities or mental telepathy and to those in the general public who still use the stylized symbolic codebooks that have been around for centuries to play the numbers, bet on horse races, or foretell the future. Such unsavory associations do not lead to a general mystique about dreams.

But a new mystique of dreams has nonetheless taken hold in the United States over the past fifteen years, a mystique that is as old as the human race in some respects, but very new and very American in others. It is a mystique that sees dreams as a source of creativity and imagination and as a ba-

sis for interpersonal closeness and social insights. It is a view
of dreams that came into popularity as one small strand of
the human potential movement of the 1960s, but since then it
has grown to the point where it is now a separate movement
with its own in-group vocabulary, books and bulletins, and
even workshops, institutes, and meeting places. Books on
"creative dreaming" and "dream power," often invoking the
wisdom of other cultures and classical Greece, have sold in
the hundreds of thousands, and science fiction stories like
The Kin of Ata Are Waiting for You and *The Word for World Is
Forest,* based on mythical nonaggressive cultures that spend
most of their time dreaming, are widely read and discussed.[5]

Several different theories and traditions have contributed
to the growth of this "dreamwork," as the movement is
usually called. They include the Swiss psychiatrist Carl
Jung's theory of dreams as a source of wisdom and personal
growth as well as the Gestalt therapist Frederick (Fritz)
Perls's belief that the emotional experiencing and dramatization of dreams by members of encounter groups can lead
to the creative integration of the personality. The beliefs
and practices of various Native American groups, as well as
the general use of dreams in spiritual healing by tribal peoples all over the world, have also been a starting point for
the new dreamwork.

Moreover, the movement has as its backdrop research on
dreams that emerged from physiology laboratories in the
1950s. This "new biology of dreaming" linked dreams to a
particular stage of sleep and to numerous behavioral and
physiological changes, including eye movement patterns,
that suggested dreams are often "watched" by the dreamer
even as they unfold. This dream stage of sleep was found to
occur in a regular pattern throughout the night, and some
studies suggested that people become nervous or upset if deprived of it. These studies gave a material reality to what hith-
erto had appeared to be an ephemeral and irregular phe-

nomenon and reinforced the inclination to believe that dreams are somehow of deep and fundamental importance.[6]

In addition to these established theories and such objective research, there is one aspect of the new mystique of dreams that is particularly fascinating and compelling to those caught up in its spirit. This is the aspect known as "Senoi dream theory," said to derive from a small tribal group by that name. According to this dream theory, the sharing of dreams can lead to heightened creativity, improved mental health, and even a more peaceful and cooperative culture. Moreover, the dreams themselves can be shaped or controlled to bring about these benefits. These were indeed powerful new claims to be made about dreams; they stirred up the age-old feelings of mystery and wonderment about them that so often have led to their veneration.

My first aim in this book is to explore the origin, appeal, and efficacy of Senoi dream theory as a principal ingredient in the new mystique of dreams. I draw upon the findings of both anthropologists and dream researchers in order to understand Senoi dream theory and its applications. I use biographical sources and describe the spread of these new ideas in order to explain their appeal. I analyze the ways in which this new mystique of dreaming corresponds to fundamental American beliefs about human nature, and I examine independent sources of evidence on the usefulness of Senoi dream principles.

However, I have a second aim as well. The story of Senoi dream theory provides a springboard for consideration of more general issues in the study of both dreams and other cultures. This is an inquiry into the sociology of an idea. It looks at the intersection of biography, history, and cultural beliefs and provides an occasion for assessing what we really know about dreams.

Just what is this Senoi way of dreaming, and who are the people who are said to practice it? According to the literature of the Jungian-Senoi Institute in Berkeley, one of the many expressions of the new mystique of dreams: "Senoi dream-work emphasizes the deliberate alteration of dream states, the resolution in dreams of problems encountered in waking consciousness, dream 'rehearsal' for activity while awake, and the application of dreams to creative individual and community projects."[7] It is a theory, then, that sees dreams as an open and positive phenomenon that can be shared and shaped for maximum human development.

The people who are thought to practice this new way of thinking about and using dreams are an aboriginal people who live in the jungle highlands of West Malaysia. Numbering between 20,000 and 30,000 in all, they live up and down isolated river valleys in loose-knit settlements of fifteen to 100 people. They practice a form of slash-and-burn agriculture as they move from site to site every few years. They hunt small game with blowpipes, gather fruits and berries, and fish with traps and baskets when they are not taking care of their fields.

The Senoi are an easygoing and nonviolent people. Their ideas about dreams are so appealing because they are believed by many dream psychologists to be among the healthiest and happiest people in the world. There is said to be no mental illness or violence precisely because they have a theory of dream control and dream utilization unlike anything ever heard of in Western history.

The main source on the Senoi use of dreams is the work of the late Kilton Stewart, who first learned about the Senoi during a stay in 1934 in what is now Malaysia. His articles in *Complex* and *Mental Hygiene* provide the basis for the discussion of the Senoi in such widely read dream books as Calvin Hall's *The Meaning of Dreams* (1953) and Ann Faraday's *Dream Power* (1972) and *The Dream Game* (1974).[8] Moreover, three different articles in *Psychology Today,* one in 1970, another in 1972, and a final one in 1978, discuss his work in a favorable light.[9] Then, too, his 1951 article, "Dream Theory in Malaya," has been reprinted in such well-known collections on human possibilities as Charles Tart's *Altered States of Consciousness* (1969) and Theodore Roszak's *Sources* (1972).

The second source for these beliefs is the work of psychologist Patricia Garfield, author of the best-selling *Creative Dreaming* (1974). Although her book has chapters on the dream practices of Native Americans, ancient Greeks, and Eastern mystics, it is in fact built around her chapter on how to learn and utilize what are said to be Senoi principles for controlling dreams. Garfield visited with some Senoi at the aborigine hospital in Gombak, Malaysia, in 1972. Until Faraday stayed for many months with Senoi groups in 1982–83, Garfield was the only dream researcher besides Stewart claiming direct knowledge of Senoi dream practices.

According to Stewart: "The Senoi make their dreams the major focus of their intellectual and social interest, and have solved the problem of violent crime and destructive economic conflict, and largely eliminated insanity, neurosis, and psychogenic illness." Although highly cooperative, they are nonetheless individualistic and creative, with each person developing his or her unique personality characteristics. As Stewart puts it in a particularly well-turned phrase: "The freest type of psychic play occurs in sleep, and the social acceptance of the dream would therefore constitute the deepest possible acceptance of the individual."[10]

Most of all, Senoi have near-perfect mental health. "Perhaps the most striking characteristic of the Senoi is their extraordinary psychological adjustment," says Garfield. "Neurosis and psychosis as we know them are reported to be nonexistent among the Senoi," she continues. "Western therapists find this statement hard to believe, yet it is documented by researchers who spent considerable time directly observing the Senoi. The Senoi show remarkable emotional maturity."[11]

Those who write about the Senoi accept Stewart's claim that this unusual level of health and happiness can be attributed to the way in which the Senoi use and interpret dreams. "There are no well-controlled scientific studies to prove that peacefulness, cooperativeness, and creativeness, mental health, and emotional maturity are the result of the Senoi's unique use of dream material," Garfield admits. "However, there is much to strongly suggest that, at the very least, their use of dreams is a basic element in developing these characteristics."[12]

For the Senoi, life is a veritable dream clinic. The concern with dreams begins at the break of day. "The Senoi parent inquires of his child's dream at breakfast, praises the child for having the dream, and discusses the significance of it," reports Stewart. "He asks about past incidences and tells the child how to change his behavior and attitude in future dreams. He also recommends certain social activities or gestures which the dream makes necessary or advisable."[13]

The dreamwork continues after breakfast at the village council. "Here the serious work of dream discussion continues," says Garfield, picking up the story. "The men, adolescent boys, and some of the women share their dreams with the larger group. They discuss the significance of each dream symbol and situation. Each council member expresses his opinion of its meanings. Those of the tribe who agree on the meaning of a dream will adopt it as a group project."[14]

The frank discussion of dreams is especially important in the promotion of social harmony. Negative actions in dreams are discussed with the people who were part of these interactions in order to resolve the problems that might have caused these images. "If the dreamer injures the dream images of his fellows or refuses to cooperate with them in dreams," writes Stewart, "he should go out of his way to express friendship and cooperation on awakening, since hostile dream characters can only use the image of people for whom his good will is running low." By the same token, "if the image of a friend hurts him in a dream, the friend should be advised of the fact, so he can repair his damage or negative dream image by friendly social intercourse."[15]

But the Senoi, it is claimed, not only share and interpret their dreams. Even more important, they shape and control them. They are able to have the kinds of dreams they want to have, free of fearful chases and frightening falls, and full of sensuality and creativity. They do so through three basic principles that are taught to children as they report their dreams around the breakfast table. These principles, which are unique in the dream literature and greatly appeal to modern readers, can be paraphrased from Stewart and Garfield as follows:

1. Always confront and conquer danger in dreams. If an animal looms out of the jungle, go toward it. If someone attacks you, fight back.

2. Always move toward pleasurable experiences in dreams. If you are attracted to someone in a dream, feel free to turn the attraction into a full sexual experience. If you are enjoying the pleasurable sensations of flying or swimming, relax and experience them fully.

3. Always make your dreams have a positive outcome and extract a creative product from them. Best of all in this regard, try to obtain a gift from the dream images, such as a poem, a song, a dance, a design, or a painting.[16]

These accounts of the Senoi people and their use of dreams have an otherworldly, utopian quality about them. They seem almost too good to be true. Indeed, Stewart's 1951 article, "Dream Theory in Malaya," begins by talking about a hypothetical "flying saucer from another planet" that lands on a "lonely mountain peak" in Malaysia. After playing with the image for another sentence or two by noting that we would be curious about the people who could make such a craft, he then turns the tables by telling us that in 1934: "I was introduced to an isolated tribe of jungle folk, who employed methods of psychology and interpersonal relations so astonishing that they might have come from another planet." Stewart thus moves from "outer space" to "inner space" in such a way that the reader is prepared to be enchanted by these fascinating people:

If you heard further that the navigators of the ship had found a group of 12,000 people living as an isolated community among the mountains, and had demonstrated that these preliterate people could utilize their methods of healing and education, and reproduce the society from which the celestial navigators came, you would probably be more curious about these psychological and social methods that conquered space inside the individual, than you would about the mechanics of the ship which conquered outer space.[17]

Mention of flying saucers, other planets, and outer space gives Stewart's article a literary quality. In fact, the more one contemplates how really remarkable and atypical these people are, the more one is likely to ask—how much of this is true? Could such healthy and happy people really exist, and if they do, are their principles of dream control and their practices of dream sharing actually the basis for their wonderful culture and superb mental health?

I will attempt to answer these questions about the Senoi and their dream theories, questions that spring from our amazement about their dream practices and their mental health. What are the Senoi like, and how did Kilton Stewart come to study and learn of their practices? Why did Senoi dream ideas suddenly have great currency in the sixties when they had been around since 1951? Does Senoi dream theory work for Westerners?

In Chapter 2, I examine the anthropological literature on the Senoi that began to appear in the late sixties but did not come to the attention of dream investigators. I also report on interviews and correspondence with the anthropologists who have spent the most time with the Senoi over the past twenty years. I discuss Senoi dream theory and practice as observed by three anthropologists who learned the language and lived among the people at different times and places in the sixties and seventies.

In order to understand how Stewart came to study the Senoi and their dream practices, I chronicle his life and work in Chapter 3, drawing on autobiographical material and biographical accounts of Stewart written in the thirties, as well as my own interviews and correspondence. I will also include an analysis of his unpublished dissertation and a comparison of it with his published writings on the Senoi.

In Chapter 4, I trace the spread of Senoi dream practices in the United States in the sixties and seventies as a basis for explaining their attraction. I describe how Senoi ideas prospered within the context of the larger human potential movement that had its primary basis at Esalen Institute near Big Sur, California. And I explain why the central precepts of Senoi dream theory appeal to American beliefs about human nature.

In Chapter 5, I assess the efficacy of Senoi dream principles by bringing together the findings of research in which the sharing or shaping of dreams has been studied in classrooms, dream groups, sleep laboratories, and other cultures. Stressing that the efficacy of Senoi dream principles is a question quite separate from their origins or their appeal, I also discuss the adequacy of the studies that are presented in the light of the social-psychological factors that are said to make Senoi dream theory actually work.

In Chapter 6, I suggest the morals that can be drawn from contemplating this tale. Here, I wax pontifical about dreams and our beliefs about dreams, discussing the major findings on dreams and the obstacles to studying them in order to provide a context for judging the contributions made by Senoi dream theory.

It is of course tempting to summarize the major findings and conclusions at this point, but to do so in advance might spoil a good detective story. Perhaps it will be more interesting if the reader learns the answers in the same order in which I struggled to them.

2

The Senoi and
Their Dream Theory

Senoi means "human being" or "person" in the language of
an aboriginal people who still manage to practice their traditional way of life in the mountainous central area of mainland
Malaysia (West Malaysia). The people called the Senoi by
dream researchers are actually two groups, the Temiar and
the Semai, who are very closely related culturally. There is
sometimes a little mutual suspicion between the Temiar and
the Semai, but there is also a considerable amount of interaction and intermarriage in some regions of the jungle.

Senoi groups are most readily distinguishable from their
neighbors by their practice of a shifting form of agriculture
in which they prepare new fields every three or four years
within those areas that are more or less theirs by tradition
and common consent. In some parts of the jungle interiors
their settlements border on the traditional areas of a few
thousand seminomadic hunters and foragers called the Se-
mang. At the edges of the jungle Senoi groups mingle with
aboriginal or proto-Malays, who are traditional farmers.
These three general groupings of native peoples share many
concepts and beliefs in common, including many beliefs
about dreams. There has also been a great deal of interbreed-
ing over the centuries, but their cultures are distinctive
enough that they appear to be defined at least in part by an

attempt to remain different from each other and to retain a
unique style of life.[1]

It seems likely that these three native cultures were pushed
off their original lands as many as 4,000 years ago by people
who came from the south of China and became what are today called Malaysians. These modern Malaysians make up
about half of the current population of West Malaysia, with
overseas Chinese comprising another one-third and Indians
and Pakistanis another 10 percent.[2] In a country of nearly 9
million, the aboriginal populations are truly miniscule, and
they must be seen first of all as conquered people.

Indeed, the Senoi are called "saki" by the Malaysians, which
means "bestial aborigine" or "slave."[3] Until the turn of the
century, when the British finally put a stop to the practice,
Senoi often were captured by Malaysians and sold as slaves. In
the past twenty-five years the government seems to have
adopted a very enlightened attitude toward the Senoi and the
other indigenous groups, but their members still remain sus-
picious of Malay intentions and government practices.

There is considerable physical isolation and cultural varia-
tion among Semai and Temiar groups. Most Senoi are unlikely to travel more than a few dozen miles from their place
of birth. The Semai speak forty different dialects. Because it
is so difficult to cross the rain forests and mountains, most
contacts are among villages along one of the several rivers
that run east and west from the highlands. There are more
frequent contacts at the headwaters in the somewhat more
open highlands, and these areas are seen as the purest regions
of Senoi culture.

Very little was published about Senoi culture until the
1960s, and most came from travelers or anthropologists on
relatively brief visits. Since then several anthropologists have
settled among Senoi peoples and have become fluent in their
difficult language, which is part of the Austro-Asiatic family
that includes Cambodian and some of the languages spoken

by Vietnamese hill people. Robert Dentan, when a student in anthropology at Yale University, spent seven months in 1962 in a mixed settlement of Temiar and Semai. He also lived with other Semai for another seven months in 1963 and returned for a brief stay in 1975. The British anthropologist Geoffrey Benjamin, who trained at Cambridge University, lived among the Temiar for eighteen months in 1964–65 and on several occasions since. Clayton Robarchek, who trained at University of California, Riverside, lived with the Semai in two different settlements for fourteen months in 1973–74 and visited them again in 1980. It is from the work of these anthropologists that we have our primary information about Senoi culture and their dream practices.

The Temiar and Semai live in loose-knit settlements of from fifteen to 100 people. In the most remote areas, where the dangers from wild elephants and tigers seem greatest, the settlement often consists of a single "long house" with compartments for a dozen or more families as well as a communal area. However, in other areas there are usually two or three smaller houses, and the number varies over the space of several months as people move into the village or depart. Built on wooden poles from four to twenty feet above the ground, the houses are made out of bamboo and are covered with thatched jungle palms.

Historically, the material culture of the Senoi was built around bamboo. "To describe the material culture of the Temiars," says H. D. "Pat" Noone, the first anthropologist to study the Senoi at any length in the 1930s, "is to tell the uses to which bamboo may be put." Bamboo is indispensable for "houses, household utensils, vessels, tools, weapons, fences, baskets, waterpipes, rafts, musical instruments and ornaments."[4]

The primary concern of the Senoi are their fields, which are "owned" by the families that clear them. It takes from two weeks to a month to clear a new field, which then will be used for two or three years in most areas before it is allowed to return to jungle. The Senoi plant a mixture of tapioca, manioc, maize, and hill rice, along with vegetables and a few fruit trees. Little time is spent in weeding the field or keeping it free of pests, almost hopeless tasks in the jungle in any case, and much of the harvest is lost to the elements and predators.

Although the Senoi obviously love their fields, they also delight in the hunt. Hunting is done with poisonous darts, which are shot out of eight-foot bamboo blowpipes. Blowpipes are sources of great pride among Senoi men. They are decorated and polished with great care and affection; more time is spent in fashioning the perfect blowpipe than in building a new house. Dentan believes that blowpipes are clearly a symbol of virility for Senoi males.[5]

The objects of a Senoi hunt are such relatively small animals as squirrels, monkeys, and wild pigs. Returning hunters are greeted with enthusiasm and gleeful dancing, and the meat is shared equally with everyone in the settlement. Although they subsist in good part on their crops and fruits, the Senoi say they have not really eaten unless the meal includes fish, meat, or fowl.

Senoi women are largely responsible for looking after the children and taking care of household chores. They also spend time making baskets and mats, gathering fruit in the jungle, helping with the fields, and fishing with baskets. There is no rigid division of labor and no strong taboos upon women during pregnancy or menstruation, but women do most of the cooking, and men usually take the leadership roles in healing ceremonies or village councils.[6]

Stewart reports that the Senoi have a peaceful way of life, and other Americans and Europeans who have spent time with them have found their culture extremely attractive. Noone, who introduced Stewart to the Senoi, married a Temiar woman; and P. D. R. Williams-Hunt, a British colonial officer who wrote a book on the aborigines of Malaysia in 1952, married a Semai woman.

The Senoi are extremely tolerant, sexually permissive, and unaggressive. Couples move slowly and informally into permanent relationships that involve no elaborate marriage ceremonies, children are deeply cared for, and there is no rigid system of religious beliefs and rituals. The Senoi prefer withdrawal to conflict, and they are not ashamed to admit when they are afraid. Reserved to the point of timidity with strangers, including other Senoi they do not know, in the company of friends they love to discuss and argue with great rhetorical flourishes. They are quick with puns and put-ons, and they use self-deprecation with great finesse in arguments. The Senoi have an open-minded perspective that Dentan characterizes as skeptical, eclectic, and pragmatic.[7]

However, it is not true that they are never violent or that their physical and mental health is exceptional. In fact, interactions with the dominant culture have led the Senoi into violent activities. Some Temiar, for example, used to guide slave raiders to Semai and other Temiar settlements, knowing that the raiders would murder many of the adults.[8] During the British-Malaysian guerrilla war with Chinese communists in the 1950s, many Temiar were members of the counterinsurgency unit called Senoi Praak, or War People. Organized in good part by Richard Noone, the younger brother of Pat Noone, they played a role in the fighting, which included some killing.[9] Similarly, Dentan reports that the Semai told him of fighting in Senoi Praak:

For example, Semai say that when they were recruited into the Malaysian government's counterinsurgency forces during the Communist uprisings of the 1950's, they were fiercer than people from other ethnic groups, partly in reprisal for terrorist acts committed against Semai. Some former troops say, "We were drunk on blood."[10]

Closer to home, the Senoi on rare occasions become violent in dealing with frustrated love or passion. Ironically, it was learned in the late fifties by Richard Noone that his brother Pat was the victim of a violent love triangle. When Pat refused to let his Temiar wife and his adopted young Temiar brother sleep together, which would not be that unusual among the Senoi, the young man eventually murdered Noone with a dart shot from a blowpipe.[11] Pat Noone himself certainly did not share the opinion that the Temiar were never violent. Rightly or wrongly, he made the following assertion based on his several months of observations and discussion in Temiar settlements:

A husband whose wife has run away and is living permanently with another man may either revenge himself indirectly by gaining the aid of a sorcerer or directly by blowpiping or spearing the man who has supplanted him.[12]

As for the Semai, Dentan also notes crimes of passion: "At least two murders have been committed between 1955 and 1977, and there is gossip about a couple of others." Nor does the relative lack of violence mean a lack of quarrels and threats. The fact that the Senoi are nonviolent does not mean they are gentle and benign, as Dentan explains:

No Semai, and no one who has spent much time with Semai, thinks of them that way [as gentle]. For example, Semai backbiting, which is frequent, is almost a dramatic art. Six months in a Semai settlement will see at least three or four serious quarrels in which voices are raised and threats of physical violence are at least alleged, if not actually made.[13]

Sickness and mental illness are hardly absent from the Temiar and Semai people. The jungle is described like a Garden of Eden by both Stewart and Garfield, but it is in fact a harsh taskmaster that takes its toll on Senoi health. The climate is extremely hot and damp, malaria is rampant in most areas, and there are numerous dangerous insects, leeches, worms, and poisonous plants. Until recently, most babies died in the first year, and many young children contract malaria or a serious respiratory disease. According to Noone, the Temiar do not give children a formal name until their second or third year, when they are sure the child is going to live. They say that this will make it easier for them to forget if the child dies and they will not be so sad.[14]

Unlike most human populations, there are more males than females in every adult age group. Alan Fix, a physical anthropologist who studied the Senoi in the late sixties, suspects that this is because so many women die in childbirth, but he cannot support this explanation with certainty because of the problems of gathering reliable data. However, the wide prevalence of hookworm infestation, which is very dangerous for pregnant women, is an indirect piece of evidence for this suspicion.[15]

There is also mental illness among the Senoi. Dentan reports as follows: "Robarchek (1977) and I (Dentan, 1968), who collected case histories, both have the impression that in most Semai settlements there will be one to three people whom we and most of the people in the settlement think are crazy."[16]

These anthropological observations are supported by the experience of a psychiatrist and medical director at the aborigine hospital in Gombak, a small town several miles from the jungle. Among twenty aboriginal psychiatric patients seen there in the course of a year in the early seventies, nine were Senoi, and all nine were psychotic. The patients were brought to the hospital in each case by relatives who had become concerned about their disruptive and unpredictable behavior. In keeping with the nonaggressiveness of the Senoi, the most frequent symptoms of these patients were withdrawal and running away. They were not likely to be aggressive, and only one, a manic depressive, had suicidal thoughts. Generally speaking, the schizophrenic patients were strikingly similar in their symptom patterns to those seen in Western societies.[17]

Illness and psychiatric problems aside, it must be remembered that the Senoi way of life is not entirely carefree and of their own choosing. As people who were forced to live in the most remote jungles if they wanted any autonomy, they are in many ways subjugated, and as such they have the mixture of admiration and fear toward their more powerful neighbors that is found in many people in their situation. They adopt a cautious and passive style toward outsiders in order to make the best of a difficult situation.

The Senoi are taught very early in life to fear outsiders. When strangers approach a village, parents yell "fear, fear" to their children and cover the heads of the infants they are holding. Although it was known up and down the valley that he was harmless, Dentan reports that when he approached, some mothers nonetheless did this with their infants merely as an object lesson.[18] Similarly, Robarchek notes that this practice made it very difficult for him to approach children even after he had been there for some time: "I was constantly thwarted in my attempts to establish contact with infants and small children by mothers who, even after we had lived in the village for months, would snatch them away and cry 'afraid.'"[19]

Children also learn to be extremely frightened through the behavior of their parents during the violent thunderstorms that suddenly and unexpectedly occur from time to time. These storms bring with them almost continuous crashes of thunder, winds of up to forty or fifty miles an hour, and the danger of flooding even for settlements on high ground. Senoi adults become very upset during these storms, sometimes running wildly into the jungles. They scream and shout, and they yell "fear, fear" to their children.[20]

According to what Semai informants told Dentan and Robarchek, these storms are the product of "Thunder," a spiritual entity who sends them because he is angry over some misbehavior or another by the Senoi. In order to appease him, people sometimes slash themselves with a bamboo knife or machete, collect the blood in bamboo containers filled with water, and then toss the mixture into the wind, shouting *terlaid, terlaid,* which means they have acted "in a way that might bring on a natural calamity."[21]

In Robarchek's observation, however, the people most frequently blame the storm on the misbehavior of children. During the storm adults seek out children and ask them what wrong they have done to cause such a calamity. When the guilty child is found, a piece of his or her hair is cut off and burned as a kind of sacrifice to Thunder. "Often," reports Robarchek, "hair from all the children is burned just in case they may have unknowingly committed some 'terlaid' offense." Robarchek believes that these practices teach children to fear their emotions and seek control of them:

When a severe storm occurs, it is the children who are questioned about and forced to reflect upon their actions. This interrogation, taking place in the fear-charged atmosphere of the storm, serves to impress further upon the children their responsibility for maintaining emotional control, for not to do so endangers the entire community.[22]

As children grow older, the concept of *terlaid* is used to restrain them in other contexts. The Senoi claim they do not instruct their children; to do so might make them sick or cause their souls to flee. Nor do they discipline children in any physical way except by carrying them back to their houses if the annoying behavior persists. However, they do yell *terlaid* when children become too loud or boisterous. They tell children there are various kinds of "bogeymen" who come in the night to cut off people's heads. Children also learn of ubiquitous "evil spirits" that often take the form of tigers or other dangerous creatures.[23]

Perhaps it is not surprising, then, given the historical situation in which the Senoi find themselves and the way in which children are raised, to learn that the Senoi people are not merely nonviolent but, in general, very restrained. After commenting on their lack of interpersonal violence or overt hostility, Robarchek notes that this is but one aspect of a general emotional reserve:

This is, however, only one manifestation of what is perhaps the most fundamental feature of Semai temperament: a low level of emotionality in general. With the exception of fearful behavior, emotional outbursts seldom occur. In addition to the virtual absence of strong expressions of anger, mourning is subdued, expression of joy is muted, and even laughter is restrained. Low affective involvement is characteristic of interpersonal relationships as well. . . . One sees few overt expressions of affection, empathy, or sympathy.[24]

This resistance to strong emotions is also seen in the fact that the Senoi will even deny being angry. "The Semai do not say, 'Anger is bad,'" writes Dentan. "They say, 'we do not get angry,' and an obviously angry man will flatly deny his anger."[25]

It seems likely, then, that Senoi psychology is more complex and typically human than the impression conveyed by Stewart and Garfield. But is there such a thing as Senoi dream theory? And what do the Senoi do with their dreams?

The Senoi do have a dream theory, and dreams are far more important in their culture than in any Western society. However, the Senoi theory is not psychological in the way that Stewart claimed, and it does not have the practical applications that he suggested. The account that follows is based primarily on Dentan's fieldwork in the mixed Temiar-Semai settlement in 1962 and the Semai settlement in 1963, supplemented by the writings of Robarchek and personal communications from Benjamin and Robarchek.

Given the variations in Senoi beliefs from river valley to river valley and the subtlety of the concepts involved, it has been far more difficult for anthropologists to understand Senoi dream theory than Senoi daily life. Nevertheless, some commonality has emerged in what anthropologists have learned about Senoi views on the psyche and dreams.

The Semai with whom Dentan discussed the nature of the psyche seem to have five basic concepts covering the entities that make up the personality.[26] Benjamin found among the Temiar he spoke with that these may reduce to two "souls" that are linked in a complex and interactive fashion.[27] Either way, the Semai and Temiar agreed that the two most important psychic entities, one localized behind the center of the forehead, the other focused in the pupil of the eye, are able to leave the body when a person is asleep or in a trance. It is these two psychic entities that account for dreaming, as Noone and Stewart suggested.

Dreams, then, are the experiences that one or the other of these "souls" has when it encounters other souls belonging to animals, trees, waterfalls, people, or supernaturals. *Ruwaay*, the soul at the center of the forehead, is by far the more important of the two when it comes to dreaming and is sometimes referred to as the "dream soul" by the Temiar.[28] *Ruwaay* appear in dreams as birds, butterflies, homunculi, or children. All *ruwaay* are timid, childlike, and a little irrational. The "soft" *ruwaay* of children are so easily frightened that the slightest thing can scare them off. Sometimes wandering *ruwaay* are so fearful of malevolent entities that they can only be lured back by special healing ceremonies called "singing ceremonies."[29] Although this theory of dreaming may not be credible to psychologically oriented Americans, it would not seem strange to many tribal people around the world. The oldest and most widespread theory of dreaming is that it is the actual experience of the soul or self while the body is asleep.[30]

Dreams can be important in many different ways in Senoi culture. They can reveal that a woman is pregnant or why a child is sick. They can tell a man whether or not his new field will be productive. Dreams are essential in contacting the supernatural world, and they play a role in healing ceremonies. It is even claimed that dreams can predict the weather. Still, most Senoi are very reluctant to make very many predictions on the basis of their dreams. They tend not to mention a predictive dream to anyone until the prediction has come true. "Thus," says Dentan, "no one ever told us about having a weather forecast dream until after the prophesied weather had occurred."[31]

For all this emphasis on dreams, the Semai and Temiar with whom Dentan lived attached no importance to most dreams. Like many Western dream theorists, the ancient Greeks, and other tribal societies with a strong interest in dreams, they discriminate between "little" dreams and "big" dreams, dreams that are insignificant and dreams that are important.[32] Insignificant dreams are *piypuuy*. They involve no contact with friendly or evil supernatural spirits, and they are generally meaningless. Obvious wish-fulfillment dreams are always *piypuuy*. "You dream of sleeping with a pretty girl and the next day you don't even see her," complained a Temiar dream expert in explaining this point to Dentan.[33]

Typical dreams, such as falling dreams, are *piypuuy*. "Kids always dream about falling. They usually grow out of it," one person explained. Another person said: "It's like dreams about fighting or burning someone's house down. It never happens. Anyway, the child usually wakes up before he hits the ground."[34]

When frightening sex dreams occur, one person claimed, the best thing to do is tell your spouse or lover about it so the alien dream soul will be too embarrassed to return. This places the blame for the dream on the dream soul of somebody else. Others deal with such dreams in an emotional way that might occur in any society; for example, a young woman and her new husband told Dentan the following:

WOMAN: About three weeks after we were married, I dreamed he'd married another woman. I lay half awake, crying and crying, until he woke me up and asked what was wrong. I hugged him and told him, crying and crying.

MAN: The first few weeks we were married, I was always dreaming she didn't love me, that she was chasing after other men. But then I decided it was because I was just a little bit jealous, so I didn't believe them.

WOMAN: When I dream he's dead or with another woman, I wake him up to tell me it isn't true.

And, just as many people do the world over, the Senoi often deny that upsetting dreams reflect their own desires. The following dialogue took place in the Semai language in 1962. Merloh is a man in his forties:

MERLOH: I dreamed last night a huge python was in my father's house. I was sitting on a log by the hearth and saw it over my shoulder, like this. I yelled "Dad, dad, come hit this python!" He came over and hit it, and it shrunk until it was tiny. . . . People in the old days would say that was the dream soul of incest.

DENTAN: You mean, you wanted to commit incest?

MERLOH: Hey, it's not *my* dream soul! Someone else is thinking about incest. Anyway, if the python is killed in the dream, the incest dream soul is killed, so you don't have to worry that it'll get you later. . . . Maybe if someone else had a dream like that, it'd be his own dream soul wanting incest.[35]

But incest dreams are not automatically threatening. One Semai explained to Robarchek that the actions and experiences of the *ruwaay* soul do not always have to be taken seriously because it is so often childlike or irrational. Dreams are often silly or trivial precisely because the *ruwaay* soul is the childish and somewhat irrational part of us.[36]

Nor are ordinary dreams seen as particularly positive. When Dentan asked one Semai what he dreamed about most often, he said "falling, stabbing people, swimming, fleeing, and dying." But he added that the dream about dying meant that he would live for a long time.[37]

The important dreams that do occur from time to time have to be understood in the context of a fundamental dichotomy that exists for the Senoi within the realm of the nonmaterial. This is the dichotomy between "they that kill us" (called *mara'* by some Semai) and "those who help us" (*gunik*). In the words of Robarchek, *mara'* are "dangerous beings that may or may not have material form at any given time."[38] Included in this category are the beings that cause illness, accidents, and other misfortunes. *Mara'* are unpredictable and malevolent. They may attack at any time for no reason at all, although doing something wrong or offending a neighbor may increase the chances of being attacked.

The only protection against a *mara'* is another *mara'* who has become friendly to a person or group. Such a *mara'* is called a *gunik,* a kind of protector or familiar, and it may be called upon in times of trouble. It is precisely at this point that dreams become significant, as Stewart recognized, but not through any conscious actions or principles of dream control. Instead, it is a matter of luck or chance that a person acquires a protector through his dreams. As Robarchek explains:

A *mara'* becomes a *gunik* by coming to a person in a dream and stating his desire to make friends. One must, however, be wary of these *mara'* because they may be deceiving the dreamer in preparation for an attack upon him. The proof that a *mara'* truly wants to become a *gunik* lies in his telling the dreamer his name and giving him a song. This song becomes the property of the dreamer, who may use it to summon the *gunik*. The *gunik* may then be called upon to assist the singer and his kinsmen and co-villagers in a variety of ways, but especially in curing illnesses and warding off other kinds of attacks by *mara'* of the same type as the *gunik*. Thus, a tiger *gunik* will protect the villagers from attack by "foreign" or "stranger" tigers, and a wind *gunik* protects the hamlet from destruction by "stranger" winds.[39]

Senoi who acquire a *gunik* summon him to help by means of curative singing ceremonies that can last for as long as three consecutive nights. These ceremonies are necessary to summon *gunik* because they are shy and hard to reach. Singing, dancing, and the rhythmic striking of bamboo sticks to produce a musical accompaniment are necessary to assure the *gunik* that they are indeed welcome.

From an American point of view these ceremonies might seem to include a combination of religion, partying, flirting, and healing. They can be a time of great merriment even when someone is ill. Their most important element is the trance state in which the individual Semai or Temiar relates to the *gunik*. It is while a person is in a trance state that the *gunik* speaks through his human "father" and is sent into the body of the patient to search out the cause of illness.

The relatively few people with *gunik* thus have the ability to deal with other supernatural entities. They are often called upon for help by other members of the settlement. Dentan used the word *adepts* to describe such people; Noone and Stewart called them medicine men or shamans. It is claimed that women can become adepts and are usually better adepts than men when they do. However, female adepts are rare, supposedly because their bodies are not strong enough to withstand the rigors of trance.[40]

The presence of a melody can turn a seemingly straight-forward wish-fulfillment dream into an important dream. A Semai man whom Dentan knew in 1962 desired to sleep with a Temiar woman, but she spurned him. He moped around for a few days and then dreamed that her soul had given him a melody. It was not, he insisted, a wish-fulfillment dream like dreaming of a winning number in a lottery, which everyone knows merely reflects your desires. Instead, this was a *gunik*-type dream. "The other man has her body," he said, "but I have her dream soul."[41]

Although dreams have a central role as the medium through which *gunik* announce themselves, no researcher has encountered the morning dream clinics described by Stewart. Since the Semai and the Temiar work at tasks they choose, they do not usually wake up at the same time. Williams-Hunt, who lived among the Semai and the Temiar in the 1940s, describes the morning scene:

Before first light in the communal house people begin to stir. The fires are kicked into a glow, some of the more energetic young men seize their blowpipes and hurry off into the jungle, others remove the cats and dogs from their vantage points and huddle close up by the fires, for early mornings in the hills can be very chilly and a few souls grunt and groan, turn over and wrap themselves up more snugly in their sleeping clothes. But by half past six everyone is up. Sleeping mats and sheets are shaken out, rolled up and put away. Protesting babies are washed and fed, dogs shooed out of the house and a few hopefuls delve into the pots for a handful of rice left over from the previous night. Usually the cockroaches have got there first. Once the house is clean, everyone goes about their daily tasks. Fowls are fed, the women go down to the waterhole to fill up their bamboos and wash clothes and themselves and the men who have not gone out hunting repair blowpipes or make traps or collect firewood.[42]

More important, Dentan found that adults deny that they ever instruct children about dreaming. According to the Senoi, asserting authority makes children sick. Even trying to persuade a child to do something it does not want to do risks scaring its *ruwaay* soul, perhaps killing the child in the process. If there is one thing that seems certain to Dentan, Benjamin, and Robarchek, it is that there is no deliberate attempt to teach children principles of dream control.[43] When Dentan explained some of the principles of Stewart's theory to a young Semai man in 1962, he had the following reaction, as recorded in Dentan's field notes:

Yung thinks it might be a good way to work out the problems of several people in the community, but has never heard of such a custom and thinks the people here would not know how to do it. He says also that the dreams of Hamid, the most aggressive child in the community, are never about hitting someone but always about someone hitting Hamid.[44]

The Semai and Temiar do hold village councils from time to time in which everyone can participate regardless of age or sex. Older men tend to dominate the proceedings, however, and the discussions involve serious disputes, not dreams. The councils can go on for many hours or even several days until everyone is satisfied. Most people find them exhausting and unpleasant; therefore, only a serious threat to the whole settlement or a general quarrel can induce everyone to participate.

Councils begin with a monologue by one of the village elders, who recounts the necessity of maintaining the group's unity in spite of the present disagreement. "He emphasizes how each of the villagers depends on the others; how all must help and care for one another; how, if one is without food, the others must feed him; and so on," writes Robarchek. "Numerous instances of such assistance in the past are recounted in detail."[45]

After several more speeches in the same vein, one of the disputants presents his or her case to the group. There is great emphasis on the style with which the argument is presented, but little concern with whether or not one part of the argument contradicts another. Robarchek stresses that the councils do not involve a discussion or trial in our sense of the word. Instead, there is a repetition of the same stories by the disputants and their respective kinsmen until all emotion has been dissipated. The problem is not so much solved as it is talked to death:

The story of the dispute and all the events leading up to it is told and retold from every conceivable angle by the principals themselves and by their kinsmen. Over and over again they tell their stories, for as long as they feel the need to do so. The fact that a particular point has been successfully countered or explained (or conceded) does not inhibit the other party from pressing it again and again if he or she feels angry or jealous or unhappy about it.[46]

Finally, one of the older male leaders will express the consensus that slowly and quietly has emerged among the listeners. He will lecture one or both of the principals about their guilt in the matter, and he may assess a small fine. But half of the fine, if not all of it, will be returned to the guilty party, once again revealing the overwhelming importance of group solidarity.

Not all disputes are settled to the satisfaction of everyone concerned. In those cases, one of the people involved is likely to move to another settlement. The sparsely populated jungle terrain and the loose Senoi social structure make it very easy for those who have conflicts to avoid each other for years on end.

This account of Senoi dream practice does not include any of the unique elements reported either by Stewart or by Garfield. There is no serious discussion of dreams at breakfast or at village councils, no instruction in how to control dreams, and no evidence in the sing ceremonies that the Senoi believe dreams can be controlled. Although these conclusions are based on work in several different settlements, there are two objections that might be raised about them. First, there is the possibility that undiscovered Temiar in the most remote or isolated parts of the jungle utilize dreams in the way claimed by Stewart. Second, it might be that the Senoi have lost or forgotten these dream practices since Stewart visited in the 1930s due to the disruption of Senoi culture by the jungle war with communist guerrillas in the fifties.

But, in fact, there are no "secret" Temiar hideouts. All Temiar settlements are known because the jungles were thoroughly surveyed and mapped by the government over the past thirty years as part of its battle against the communists. Moreover, Benjamin has visited almost all of the most remote Temiar groups as part of his ongoing studies of Temiar religion, and he has found no evidence of a different use of dreams there.[47]

The possibility that Senoi culture was disrupted by the "emergency" of the fifties, as the counterinsurgency was called, has greater surface plausibility. At first, the Senoi were rounded up into a few camps in an attempt to prevent the communists from getting any help with food or information. This was a two-year internment, which led to such a high death rate among the Senoi that they were allowed to return to the jungle, with some being recruited into counterinsurgency groups as well. This experience is bitterly remembered by many Senoi, and it is still regarded by some of them as the first step in a plan to deprive them of their land.[48]

As bad as the emergency was for individual Senoi, there is no evidence that it had any lasting effect on Senoi beliefs or culture or that it erased all memory of the previous use of techniques of dream control. This is demonstrated in the observations of Iskander Carey, the anthropologist who knew the Temiar best in the middle and late fifties. In the introduction to his 1961 book on Temiar grammar, he wrote about the minimal effects of the emergency on the Temiar way of life:

As a result of the Emergency, the number of contacts between Temiar and outsiders has considerably increased, and the deep jungle areas have strategically acquired considerable importance. But neither Communist Terrorists nor the Security Forces have basically altered the Temiar way of life, and their physical isolation makes any great changes unlikely in the near future.[49]

Benjamin's first paper on the Temiar, published in 1966, similarly comments on how little the outside world had impinged on the people at that time. He notes that many of them had memories of the "old days" before either World War II or the emergency and that they did not feel things had changed.[50] This continuity is also revealed in some of Benjamin's genealogical work. He notes that part of his fieldwork was done in Ressing, one of the villages reported on by Pat Noone in his only published paper in 1936. As part of his kinship work there, Benjamin succeeded in "tracing what happened to every person on Noone's genealogy, so demonstrating its continuity with my own data."[51] Such a detailed accounting thirty years later would hardly be possible if there had been serious disruptions of the traditional social structure or if the Temiar had forgotten their past.

The continuity between the thirties and sixties is also revealed in the fact that both Dentan and Benjamin did fieldwork in the same mixed Temiar-Semai settlement where Stewart did part of his work twenty-five years earlier. Then, too, the man who "adopted" Dentan at his second field site in 1963 had been Noone's field assistant among the Temiar. Benjamin also talked with informants who had worked for or knew Noone in the thirties.[52]

How little had changed on the cultural level between the early thirties and 1974–75 when Robarchek was there can be demonstrated very concretely by comparing Pat Noone's brief section "The Spirit Element in Temiar Life" in his 1936 monograph with the description of Semai spirit and healing beliefs by Robarchek in his 1979 paper, "Learning to Fear." Noone begins: "To the Temiar the whole of nature is im-

pregnated by spiritual forces, many of them personified in
the form of evil spirits." He then describes the "medicine
man" (*hala*) who leads the singing ceremonies as an "inter-
mediary between man and the world of spirits." This "medicine man" is aided in his "combat" with "the evil spirits of
which indignant nature is full" by being in the "possession"
of his "tiger-familiar (*gunik*)." Noone then explains that the
medicine man attains a state of "dissociation" through his
dancing, in which he "forgets his own self" and "is believed
to be possessed by his *gunik* or 'familiar.'" Noone concludes:
"It is this *gunik* which makes the *hala* 'powerful to heal sickness.'"[53] Unfortunately, Noone's full account of Temiar spiritual life was never written, but the correspondence between
what little he wrote about healing ceremonies and what has
been reported by Robarchek (and Dentan and Benjamin) is
remarkable across time and settlements.

Nor did the long visit with the Senoi in 1982–83 by Faraday and her husband, John Wren-Lewis, lead to any evidence
of cultural change or loss of older dream practices. They reported that "it would be hard to imagine a people more dedi-
cated to preserving their traditions intact despite all the
changes going on around them," and they note that "our welcome would have been short-lived had we not scrupulously
observed their time-hallowed rituals and taboos." They
talked to elders who recalled the thirties, including one who
actually had told his dreams to Noone and to Stewart. Faraday and Wren-Lewis conclude:

Sadly, we must report that not a single Temiar recalled any
form of dream control education in childhood or any such
practice amongst adults; in fact they vehemently denied that
dream manipulation has ever been part of their culture. And
dreams play such an integral part in their whole religious life
that we cannot conceive of a major dream-practice being allowed to fade into oblivion when the religion itself is so very
much alive.[54]

There seems to be no way, then, to avoid a rather mundane conclusion after weighing a great deal of anthropological evidence from a variety of sources: Senoi people do not have an unusual theory or practice of dreams. What they believe and do would come as no great surprise to one of the founders of anthropology, Edward Tylor, who wrote that dreams were an important basis for a belief in a spirit world and a separable soul.[55] Nor is Senoi dream theory very different from the tribal and peasant beliefs brought together by the great psychoanalytic anthropologist Geza Roheim in his 1952 study, *The Gates of the Dream*.[56] And it would be difficult to count the number of ethnographic field reports that have commented on the use of dreams by shamans in healing ceremonies all over the world.[57] Given the unanimity of this evidence, a new question now emerges. How did the more exotic beliefs about the Senoi and their dream theory develop?

3

The Magic of Kilton Stewart

The previous discussion was based on the similar experiences and observations recorded by several anthropologists at different field sites. Their findings are at variance, however, with many of the claims of Kilton Stewart, and differences of time and location do not seem to resolve the discrepancies. It becomes necessary, therefore, to turn to a consideration of Stewart's life and work to help unravel the remaining mysteries of Senoi dream theory.

Even the barest facts about Stewart have been little known, for he did not move in the usual academic circles or publish in the typical social science journals. But even the obvious facts only hint at the full story, for Stewart was one of the most audacious and colorful people ever to espouse theory in the realms of psychology and anthropology.

Stewart was born in 1902 in Provo, Utah, where his father was the city traffic engineer. The second of six children, four boys and two girls, he graduated from high school in Provo in 1920. He spent his freshman year at Brigham Young University in 1921–22, then went to the University of Utah from 1924 to 1928 to earn his bachelor's degree. Stewart returned to the University of Utah in 1930–31 for a master's degree in psychology, and he received his Ph.D. in anthropology from the London School of Economics in 1948. He spent most of his time between 1920 and 1940 traveling around the world, and for most of the years between 1940 and 1965 he practiced psychotherapy in New York City, where he died of cancer at the age of sixty-two.

One of the people who knew Stewart best in the 1930s was a young British woman, Claudia Parsons, who met him in Southeast Asia in 1937–38 when she was halfway through a trip around the world. Parsons kept a diary of her journey, which became the basis for a charming travelogue, *Vagabondage,* published in 1941. She recorded her first impressions of Stewart when she spotted him at breakfast just before an early morning bus ride in what is now Cambodia in November 1937, comparing him with someone named Christian she had met earlier in her travels:

He had the same attractive air of devilry, the same stocky figure. But he was broader than Christian and rather older. He wore sandals on his feet, and his linen suit was that of the beachcomber hero in an American film who is either about to reform or is slowly sinking to a living death. . . . There was more than an idle curiosity in that academic forehead, in that Bible history head. One felt that John the Baptist had just caught the bus.[1]

The beachcomber hero who looked like John the Baptist was indeed striking in appearance: handsome good looks, a strong build, and powerful shoulders, the latter the products of work on his father's ranch and his love of swimming. But he was even more impressive as a conversationalist, and as he expounded "on religion, youthful repressions, personality conflicts, and finally on dreams being the expression of one's ego," Parsons learned that he considered himself a psychoanalyst. "It was early impressed on me," she continues, "that he was a follower not of Freud but of Otto Rank, having himself been psycho-analyzed by one of Rank's disciples in Paris." Parsons also heard about his interest in tribal peoples:

There was a long record of study and experience. By degrees I gathered the threads of life shared between public institutions and solitary expeditions, when he carried out research among such as the hairy Ainus of Northern Japan, the head-hunters of Formosa and the Negritos of the Philippines. Talking to Stewart one learnt that the answers to many present-day problems were to be found in the study of primitive cultures. These expeditions were financed either on public research money or out of his own fluctuating resources, but I did not then know to what extent those resources fluctuated.[2]

Following the bus ride, Parsons and Stewart spent two busy and romantic days in Bangkok. Stewart also roamed the back streets looking for ivories, jade, Oriental knives, and small antiques. Then their ways parted because Stewart was going to visit Senoi territory in what was then called Malaya. He asked Parsons to join him as the secretary-typist for the expedition. When she reluctantly refused his kind offer, Stewart professed a broken heart. But by this time Parsons had a good understanding of her new friend:

When I boarded my train I left Stewart, so he told me, with a broken heart. But I was not frightened of having damaged a heart so seasoned. And a psychoanalyst with a broken heart is a contradiction of ideas.[3]

After an exchange of letters and telegrams, however, Parsons met up with Stewart and one of his friends about two months later in Singapore. It was during the stay in Singapore that Parsons made another of those discoveries about Stewart that always left her speechless:

The last evening in Singapore is worthy of mention, when at a party at the Tanglin swimming-pool Stewart divulged that he was an elder of the Mormon Church. This was a crowning discovery. I had learnt something of the Mormon history whilst in America, of their ousting from one place after another all across the States till they made their last stand in the deserts of Utah and turned these into habitable country.

Here amongst us was a descendant of two families prominent in this history, here was Stewart with a hundred and
thirty-four first cousins and a grandfather who went to Mex-
ico rather than give up his four wives.

America now rather esteemed these law-abiding citizens,
but Stewart in a life of roaming appeared to have violated
most of the Mormon abstentions. It was now a supreme jest
that in his early years he had gone on the foreign mission that
establishes an elder. Nevertheless in five months I had time
to discover that this often exasperating companion was truly
Christian.[4]

Shortly thereafter, Stewart and Parsons decided to take an
automobile trip from Calcutta to London. Over the next
three months she learned that he possessed even more unusual traits than she had imagined. For example, he was gen-
erous to a fault, giving away money right and left:

Stewart's whole wealth was a rapidly dwindling £60 with
hope of another £20 in Cairo, but instead of pondering on the
hiatus between here and England, he was concerned only
with how to support the beggar population of the countries
through which we passed.

More than money, Stewart wanted to give everyone a ride
even though he and Parsons had only a two-seat Studebaker
with a rumbleseat in the back:

Every time I went to sleep, when I woke up there was another
pedestrian stuffed into our dinky seat, while in India I woke to
find that with our bumper rail we were pushing a large vehicle
which had run out of petrol on the road. The pedestrians that
we helped were highly varied. They wore turbans, skull-caps
or sometimes woolen caps of the Cossack type. . . . It was the
poorer, down-at-heel type whom Stewart mostly assisted. We
were a sort of good-will bus service.[5]

Parsons's warm portrait of Stewart as a zestful charmer
and open-handed traveler is filled out and supported by an

autobiographical account that he dictated to another friend, a young Australian named Nancy Grasby, just a year before he met Parsons. Entitled "Journey of a Psychologist," this unpublished manuscript recounts his adventures between 1932 and 1934. It begins with his musings after he was fired from his job at a Utah state school for mentally retarded children. Perhaps he lost his job because he kept alcohol in his room, which was against the rules. Or maybe it was because he had attempted an unauthorized experiment in curing bedwetting with a mild electroshock device. Or maybe it was both—Stewart could not decide.

The manuscript tells how he then hopped a freight train from Salt Lake to Sacramento and sold Fuller brushes in the wealthy sections of Oakland for a few months while he hung around Berkeley. Eventually he decided to move on to Honolulu, but he had to travel as a stowaway because the seaman's papers he had obtained on one of his earlier journeys around the world were not good enough to get him a legitimate ride across the ocean. The manuscript continues with his many adventures in Hawaii, reports on the roundabout way he finally obtained a job as a mental tester for the psychologist S. D. Porteus, and ends with a long account of the deliriums and fantasies caused by a bad case of what he calls typhus fever, contracted during his first trip into the jungles of Malaya.

The self-portrait of an adventurer who lived by his wits that is provided in the early parts of this youthful memoir is not a fictional product of Stewart's fertile imagination. It is supported by the recollections of two people who knew him well, his brother, Omer, and Dorothy Nyswander, a psychology professor who first met him when he was an undergraduate at the University of Utah. Omer, now retired from the University of Colorado after a distinguished career as an anthropologist that included several books and dozens of articles on the Indians of Utah and the Southwest, recalls that

Stewart first began taking unauthorized train rides as a teen-ager. By the time Stewart was in his late twenties, according to Omer, he had been around the world two or three times as a merchant seaman.[6]

The idea that Stewart was able to stowaway on a ship to Honolulu may seem unlikely, but it is corroborated by Nyswander. In the early thirties she was teaching at the University of California, Berkeley, and Stewart stayed with her when he arrived on the West Coast. Nyswander recalls being with him on the docks of San Francisco while he walked up and down, deciding which ship would be most likely to treat him well and give him a job in the kitchen once he was dis-covered.[7]

According to his own account, Stewart soon tired of his job in Honolulu. He decided he wanted to do mental testing among tribal groups in the Pacific. It was thus that he had come to visit the Ainus of Japan, the headhunters of For-mosa, the Negritos of the Philippines, and several other primitive groups.

The manuscript, however, is not primarily about his find-ings with these groups. It is also full of adventure, telling of near drownings, battles with illness, love affairs with exotic women, and encounters with such interesting characters as an aging prospector in the mountains of the Philippines and an American-turned-Buddhist priest in Bangkok. The data that he collected from his mental testing were turned over to Porteus in Honolulu and were later used as part of a chapter in Porteus's *Primitive Intelligence and Environment* (1937).[8]

Stewart dictated his 1936 manuscript because he did not like to write, and he was also an extremely poor speller. He dis-cusses these matters with his usual flair in the autobiography:

The two days of facing the unknown of the Philippines stim-ulated my literary ambition and I wrote two articles, one on the Ainus and one on the Formosans. It was my first attempt at writing since my Freshman Themes had given up their split infinitives and comma faults to the avid eyes of the English instructors, when I had vowed never to write again if the gods would give me enough "Bs" to balance up the "Ds." I felt very guilty as I broke this promise; but there is something fearsome about being a stranger in a strange land, which makes men lose sight of their standards.[9]

Once in Manila, he repaired to a park early one morning to get the articles ready to show a magazine publisher there:

I hauled out my dictionary, found a bench in the shade of a tree, and looked for the evidence of my creative urge in the line of spelling. Since early childhood I had striven to maintain individuality in this field. By four o'clock I thought I had looked up every word that I had used. I thought pleasantly of tea as I made my way to the appointment. The editor was a charming fellow, and, after scanning my articles, said that he would take them but that he would sue me if translating them ruined his spelling for life. Apparently I had missed a word here and there.[10]

Actually, the articles never appeared, and that was probably the last time that Stewart laid pen to paper. Henceforth he would dictate all of his ideas to women who believed in him and his creative abilities, relying on them to be his editors and proofreaders.

Although Stewart was not much of a writer, he had unusual talents as a speaker and storyteller, as attested to by Parsons and others. He seemed to be able to convince anyone of anything. People were enthralled by the stories he could tell from his many travels even though they didn't always believe him. "Kilton was a great story-teller and I often had the impression he would not worry about the exactness of details if it might interfere with his narrative," his brother Omer wrote to me.[11] "I never knew what to believe, but he was a wonderful friend and companion," Dorothy Nyswander told me at the outset of our interview. "Tell me," she continued, "did he really get a Ph.D. in England?"[12] One of his friends from the fifties, John Wires, a young man at the time, asked me exactly the same question after telling me how he heard Stewart speak to a liberal group at the Community Church in New York and became interested in his theories.[13]

Stewart's penchant for dramatic stories is illustrated by his account to a reporter in 1964 of how he came to be interested in dreams. Beginning with the fact that his father had been a government surveyor, Stewart said that as a boy he often went along with his father when he surveyed on Indian reservations. There he met a shaman who helped him conquer a terrifying dream:

It was a shaman medicine man who first taught me you could direct your dreams. I had a terrifying one of a coyote whose tail tickled my stomach. "That's all right," said my friend. "He's just trying to tell you that someday you will be a medicine man and will cure people. When he comes again, let him inside of you." I did and was never terrified again.[14]

According to Omer, who was very close to Kilton and very proud of his exploits, this account could not possibly be true. Their father left government surveying before Kilton was born to work for the city of Provo, and the Indians of Utah were on two reservations that were far from where the Stewart children grew up. It is Omer's strong recollection that Kilton did not spend any time with Indians until he and Omer became friends with the anthropologist Julian H. Steward at the University of Utah and helped him with his archeological work on one of the Utah reservations in the summer of 1930 or 1931. When I expressed skepticism and asked Omer how he had become interested in Indians and anthropology, he replied that it was through an introductory class in anthropology during his freshman year at the University of Utah.[15]

In addition to his rhetorical talents, Stewart also was an

excellent hypnotist. He had learned this skill on his own in the early thirties, and he had practiced it all over the world, even for minor sultans in Asia and in the context of tribal dances and healing ceremonies. He also used it to collect hypnotic dreams for some of his studies.

One of the several people able to attest to Stewart's abilities as a hypnotist is Sir Edmund R. Leach, perhaps the most distinguished anthropologist in the English-speaking world. Leach had finished a three-year contract as a commercial assistant for a British firm when he met Stewart at a party at the British embassy in Peking in 1936. It was not too long before Stewart had convinced Leach to join him and Nancy Grasby on a short expedition to study the Yami on Botel Tobago, a small, windswept island forty miles off the coast of Formosa. It was there that Leach saw Stewart put natives into a trance as part of his dream research:

He had considerable skill as a hypnotist and having seen him at work I underwent the experience myself. He put his "patient" into a very light state of hypnotic "trance" and told him to "dream" and to report what he was "dreaming." The process was very interesting; the "patient" was fully conscious of what he was saying and seeing and remembered it quite clearly afterwards. . . .

What was also very extraordinary was that he was able to carry through this hypnosis through interpreters, sometimes even a chain of interpreters. I have myself been present when a [native] was hypnotized by Stewart speaking to a Chinese who knew both English and Japanese who in turn spoke to a [native] who understood Japanese who then spoke to the "patient" who proceeded to report a very "Freudian dream" which he found so shocking that he immediately woke up.[16]

According to the 1936 autobiographical manuscript, Stewart's first visit to Senoi country was unplanned and unexpected. He had arrived in Singapore in early 1934 after completing his testing for Porteus, and he was down to his last few dollars. He was planning on a recreational week in an exciting city before catching a steamer to Hawaii:

Three luxurious days passed by, and then I began to wonder about the natives of Malay. The life of the hotel palled. In the little city of Taiping, I was told, there was the Ethnographic Museum of the Federated Malay States, and there was a man there named H. D. Noone who ate, drank and breathed natives. He even kept them in his garage. Mr. Noone was the Government Field Ethnographer. It was only a two hour ride on the train to Taiping. I asked for my bill.[17]

Noone was not at home when Stewart arrived, but his Malay servant invited Stewart to come in and wait for his return. The result was an enjoyable week of hot baths and good meals before Noone finally appeared. According to Stewart, he and Noone hit it off immediately, a claim that is easily believed because other accounts report that Noone was almost as outgoing and open-handed as Stewart. As for Noone, he took one look at Stewart and named him "Torso":

He would be delighted to have a companion in the jungle, and if I would give him an excuse of the data I would collect on mental tests he would wangle enough extra funds to bring my journey within my financial range, which I had informed him was nothing. As I protested weakly that I could hardly hope for such good fortune, he answered, "Rot. Come now and bring your torso down to lunch, and forget such sentimental twaddle. 'Torso,'" he repeated, looking at my shoulders as we sat down. "The torso of American youth straining to maintain his liberty." From then on I was "Torso."[18]

According to Stewart, the expedition started with an elephant caravan and lasted about two or three months. Noone's published paper gives a somewhat different picture, however. He calls it one of several demographic expeditions concerned with the distribution of settlements. It had a field staff of only two men and people recruited from the various settlements to serve as bearers. Noone explains that he already had spent two different three-month periods learning the Temiar language and studying Temiar culture at other settlements. He describes the expedition with Stewart:

In 1934 we (Mr. K. R. Stewart accompanied me on this expedition) started from [the town of] Lasah on my second expedition across into [the province of] Kelantin, this time taking a line further north by following the Temor [River] towards its source and so into [the] Ulu Piah [area], finding the source of the Betis [River] just by [the town of] Gunong Grah. On this occasion when I arrived after twelve marching days and two rafting days at [the town of] Kuala Betis I rafted on down the Nenggiri [River], stopping at [the town of] Kuala Jindera, and so reached Bertram, a station on the East Coast Railway—after two days of rafting.[19]

Two conclusions seem to emerge from this description and other information in Noone's monograph. First, it is not likely that they had an elephant caravan, at least beyond the first day or so. More important, it is very likely that this expedition lasted in the neighborhood of sixteen days.

Whatever the length of the trip, Stewart reports that he and Noone participated in several of the song ceremonies that were put on for their benefit, sometimes joining in the dancing or inducing the much-coveted trance states through hypnosis. Indeed, Stewart drew some conclusions about the nature of Temiar religion on the basis of his hypnotic work:

The fact that we could send them into their dance trances and call the familiars of their medicine men through hypnosis made it appear that the whole religious pattern of the group was carried through direct and indirect suggestibility, and that all religions are perpetuated from generation to generation in a similar manner.[20]

Actually, this hypothesis about the nature of religion was not an entirely new one for Stewart. He put forth a somewhat similar view in his master's thesis on religion, which is entitled "Fear as Prime Factor in the Origin of Religion." Working within a Pavlovian framework, Stewart argued that religion is based on a conditioned fear of the unknown and is then passed on through imitation. The argument is illustrated with material from a wide variety of anthropological studies. It was done under the direction of a behavioristic psychologist, M. C. Barlow, Dorothy Nyswander, who also was a behaviorist at the time, and Julian Steward.

In any case, there is only one brief mention of dreams in Stewart's 1936 account of his first visit to Senoi country. It appears in the context of the general program of his investigations with Noone:

We spent a few very pleasant days in the first long house. I gave mental tests and asked the inmates about their phantasies and dreams; Noone measured them, checked up on legends and obtained genealogies. We also instituted our programme of hypnosis. Many of the natives had slight abrasions on their skin, which we treated with various types of ointments, telling them that part of the treatment was to sit in a camp chair and look at a bright object and go to sleep. The most interesting material we got was from the medicine men, who told us in detail about the professional training they had had.[21]

Stewart left Malaya in the spring of 1934, and he did not return for three and a half years. In between, he made two different trips to Peking, spent several weeks on the aforementioned expedition to Botel Tobago, and returned to the Philippines for the third or fourth time to collect dreams in a Negrito group.

Stewart also claims to have undergone a Rankian psychoanalysis in Paris in the summer of 1935, but the particulars of his training and analysis are still lost to history despite my efforts to uncover them. Otto Rank, one of Freud's earliest and most creative followers, had broken with Freud in 1926 and set up his own school of psychoanalysis. His theory deviated widely from Freud's, putting great emphasis on the traumatic effects of the birth experience and the importance of a creative will or life spirit. He also came to believe that the lengthy treatments that had become part of psychoanalytic orthodoxy were not really necessary. His own brand of therapy became a matter of a few weeks or months, with considerable time spent in discussion of spiritual growth and little or none on childhood fears and fantasies.[22]

Rank moved to Paris in 1926 to take up private practice, and in 1934 he and his small handful of followers founded a summer institute there called the Psychological Center. The six-week session included lectures by social workers, psychiatrists, and psychologists from Paris, New York, and Philadelphia. Rank gave several of the lectures. Plans were made to hold the institute again the next summer, but they were canceled because Rank moved to New York in the fall of 1934. Rank was in Paris in the spring of 1935 for only a few weeks and then returned to New York.[23]

Nonetheless, Stewart reports in a brief biographical statement written for a family history in 1944 that he was "psychoanalyzed at the Rankian Psychoanalytic Center" in Paris in 1935 and then worked at a Psychopathic Hospital in that city. What he may have done was to work with the psychologist Pearce Bailey, who had received his Ph.D. at the Sorbonne in 1933 and helped Rank run the Psychological Center in 1934. Bailey stayed in Paris through 1936 before returning to the United States to earn a medical degree and become a neurologist.[24] But whatever Stewart's exact involvement with Rank or any of his followers, the experience clearly meant a great deal to him.

Although nothing is known about the nature of Stewart's work in Paris, some things can be inferred about its length and intensity from his travel schedule and a letter to his brother. He left New York for Paris in May or June of 1935, arrived in Paris in late June or early July, and in the fall he left Paris for a railroad trip to Peking via Eastern Europe and the Soviet Union, arriving in Peking in December 1936 or January 1937.[25] In other words, his psychoanalytic training, if he had any, may have been brief even by Rankian standards. He gives a glimpse of it in a letter to Omer from Peking dated January 22, 1936:

I guess Detroit was the last place in which I heard from you. From there I had a very triumphal march on to NYC and thense to Europe. The Analysis was most interesting and I think valuable beyond words. I am highly pleased about it. When I see you next I shall dig into you with the old fear pick. It was great fun just loafing around Paris. I never enjoyed myself more. I shacked up with an Australian actress and used her for a laboratory course in analysis. The whole stay was just about perfect. I gave all my money away to communist refugees from Germany and was delightfully broke the whole time.

The letter also makes clear that Stewart was highly impressed with Rank's theories and was using them in his work in Peking:

Arriving here I got right into the work at the Psycho Pathic Hospital and have been utterly charmed and absorbed ever since. I am working on a half dozen insane patients with psychoanalysis and hypnosis and have had two or three private patients nearly all of the time and so am getting plenty of experience. I think Rank is superb as a thinker and am planning tests all the time and have built and am trying a few of them on the patients with which I hope to put a lot of his theories to the test. So far I think he is just about as near right as anyone could be about everything.

Armed with his new theoretical perspective and his identification as a psychoanalyst, Stewart made his second visit to

Senoi country early in 1938. This trip was planned in advance, and it again included Noone, but it nonetheless had some elements of Stewart's unique style. We know a great deal about this stay, thanks to the very lucky fact that Claudia Parsons agreed at the last minute to go along as his typist if Stewart would drive to London with her afterward. She begins her report by providing us with a picture of the general setting:

Noone had chosen a convenient and not too remote Saki [that is, Senoi] village in order to work on his treatise with the subject matter right before him. For seven weeks we lived within sight of a Temiar down-river group, for seven weeks time was only indicated by night and day, by hunger and fatigue. Only my faithful reporting in my diary showed us the progress of the year.[26]

Even in a setting relatively close to civilization, however, Parsons anticipated a fair amount of hardship, but instead she was in for yet another surprise:

Jungle life was not what I had expected. I had foreseen a period of semi-darkness, a bunch of tents, boiled water to drink and little chance of washing till April. Instead I had a house of my own, hot water and early morning tea brought to me each day by a Malay servant, while beer, ginger beer, tongue, curries and a gorgonzola cheese were amongst the things that sustained me. Even a box of cigars was dissipated in the study of Temiar culture.[27]

The study moved along in an uneventful fashion. Noone and Stewart would go down to the same mixed Temiar-Semai settlement later studied by Dentan and Benjamin and then return to dictate to Parsons:

Our days were spent collecting and sorting data, while I typed to the dictation of Stewart or Noone. Stewart, who seemed to work best when in the horizontal, lay flat on a bench and gave dissertations that contained words like *physi-*

ological, palaeolithic and *schizothymic,* words that made me glad of that cushion of jungle between me and the world. For one might sack a typist in England for a mere negligence, but it would have been an awful offence or a devastating ignorance before she was sent packing on an elephant. Luckily I had my dictionary.[28]

It was the information collected on this second visit to the jungle, which ended on March 24, 1938, that provided most of the systematic Senoi data that Stewart eventually used in his dissertation.

Once in London, Stewart's thoughts turned to the possibility of earning a Ph.D. in anthropology. He had mentioned the idea in one or two letters to his family and to Omer in conversations, but this was the first time he had decided to do anything about it. Since he already had plenty of data, it was primarily a matter of organizing it into a dissertation. He initially planned to register at Cambridge University in the fall of 1938 but then decided on the London School of Economics instead.[29]

Noone also was in England in late 1938 and early 1939, on a leave from his job with the Department of Aborigines in Malaya. Stewart wrote to his family in Utah that the two of them planned to write up their findings together for publication as well as work on individual dissertations. Noone, who had first registered as a Ph.D. candidate at Cambridge in 1935 under the provisional title "The Social Psychology of the Temiar Senoi, a Jungle Tribe of Malaya," at this time changed his topic to the more specific subject of dreams. He registered his new title as "Dream Experience and Spirit Guides in the Religion of the Temiar Senoi of Malaya."[30]

Noone gave a talk based on his Senoi dream data to the Royal Anthropological Institute in March 1939. Entitled "Chinchem: A Study of the Role of Dream-Experience in Culture-Contact Amongst the Temiar Senoi of Malaya," it concerned the introduction of a new ceremonial dance called

"Chinchem." The dance had been obtained from a dream revelation by a leading adept or shaman. Although no copy of the talk exists, it is summarized in the Royal Anthropological Institute's journal, *Man* (April 1939). According to the summary, Noone argued that the new ceremonial dance arose from the difficulties this particular Temiar group was experiencing because of its contacts with Malay culture. His main claim was that the new values introduced through the dream and the dance had "mobilized the morale of this group towards more effective adjustment in the contact situation."[31]

Noone also noted that there were certain similarities between Chinchem and the ghost dance revivals among Indians in the United States in the late nineteenth century, and the parallels are indeed striking. As with his 1936 paper, Noone's findings and conclusions in this talk are ones that are consistent with what other anthropologists have observed. Thirty years later, for example, Weston LaBarre called his book on the origins of religion *The Ghost Dance* (1970). From a study of religions around the world, including the new religions that arise in the crisis situations that primitive groups face when they confront Western colonialists, LaBarre concluded that "every religion begins in some dramatic individual revelation or dream, culturally diffused to others, and gradually edited into the necessarily vague and contradictory entity appropriate to a whole group."[32]

Stewart also gave a lecture at the institute during his stay in London. It was entitled "A Psychological Analysis of the Negritos of Luzon, Philippine Islands." According to the four-paragraph summary in *Man* (January 1939), it was based on work done in two periods of three months each in the summers of 1933 and 1937. Using data from various mental tests as well as free associations under hypnosis, word associations, and dreams, Stewart concluded that "a rough analysis of the test results fails to support the theory of racial differences, as there were individuals in all three groups [of Negritos] who compared favourably with the higher test scores of Europeans." Stewart put his findings into the context of his theoretical interest in Otto Rank. The summary concluded:

An attempt was made to interpret all this material according to the general theories of psychotherapy and psychoanalysis. The terminology and ideology of Otto Rank seemed to be the most useful in unifying the various phenomena. These data also argued for the similarity of the intellectual and emotional natures of different racial strains of humanity.[33]

The talk is notable for the absence of any hint of superior and inferior races. At a time when many test-oriented psychologists believed that preliterate people were less intelligent than Europeans and Americans, Stewart believed just the opposite. His convictions were all the more impressive because of the teachings of the Mormon church.

In fact, Stewart was a strong egalitarian and a critic of capitalism as well. His letter to Omer from Peking in January 1936, following his trip across the Soviet Union, included the following paragraph on his impressions of that country:

Russia was intensely stimulating and if I had not already been pretty sold on their expierment I think I should have been wone over 100% at that time. My god how they are doing things. They are an nation full of hope and courage. No unemployment and food prices steadily on the decline and every day a greater belief in their own destiny. They are doing a magnificent job.[34]

In a paper he published a year later in the *Philippine Magazine* on "The Yami of Botel Tobago," Stewart used his findings on the Yami to make a sustained critique of racism and inequality. After noting that casual observers might think these people are "stupid savages" because their level of material development is so primitive, he attacks that kind of argument on the basis of his test results:

Such a conclusion, however, would prove the observers more stupid than they think the Yami are, for, in fact, these simple folk are neither stupid nor savage. During a three-month expedition among them which has just been completed, their performances in various mental tests indicate them to be quite on a par intellectually with Chinese, Japanese, and European-American norms, and an examination of their social system makes it appear that they are from many viewpoints less savage than any of the great groups who pride themselves so highly on their civilization.[35]

Stewart contrasts the equality of the Yami social order with the extremes of wealth and power in modern capitalist societies:

It makes it appear that what we have been calling capitalism is nothing more than industrial feudalism, and that feudalism is a mental disease, which destroys both the master and the serf. When a man thinks himself to be a god and starts killing devils, we put him in an insane asylum, at least we still do in some countries. But when he thinks he creates a railroad or a bridge or a skyscraper, because of some circumstance which enables him to direct or initiate the work, we put his name in the foundation stone and make him a feudal baron. Most of the men who employed their brain and muscle in the group enterprise get no credit for the creation. Their creative work is traded for the right to live, sold over the block for the profit of others.[36]

In short, there are strong indications that the itinerate mental tester and would-be dream theorist also was a passionate social critic. It was an element of his character that gave an immediacy and moral force to his later writings on dreams, which are infused with calls for social betterment.

Despite their respective talks to the Royal Anthropological Institute, there are no indications that anything further materialized in the way of writing for either Noone or Stewart at this time. Noone returned to Malaya soon thereafter and was caught up in the war against the Japanese. He was killed by his Senoi rival in a love triangle while working in the jungles against the Japanese, and all his data and manuscripts were destroyed at some point by Japanese soldiers.

What more Noone had learned about the Senoi use of dreams or how he would have utilized the dreams he had collected in early 1938 may never be known with certainty. The claims about his views put forth in a book on his life by his brother Richard are romantic accounts of doubtful accuracy. They are based in good part on retrospective memory, conversations with Stewart, and Stewart's own articles. Letters that Pat Noone wrote to his parents in the early thirties demonstrate interest in the Senoi emphasis on dreams, but there is no indication in his 1936 monograph or his talk to the Royal Anthropological Institute that he shared Stewart's later claims about Senoi dream sharing and dream control.[37]

Following Noone's departure for Malaysia in 1939, Stewart wanted to stay in London, but his plans were disrupted by the war in a totally unexpected way. He happened to be visiting friends in Paris in September 1939 when the war broke out. As an American citizen he was immediately shipped directly back to the United States from France. He arrived in New York with only the few belongings he had taken with him to France. Fortunately Parsons retrieved his trunks of memorabilia and data from the apartment that one of her friends had loaned to Stewart.[38] There things stood as far as the dissertation and Senoi dream theory were concerned until after the war.

Unexpectedly relocated to the United States, Stewart settled in New York City in the early forties to practice a mixture of Rankian psychoanalysis and his own dream-based therapy. Shortly after he set up practice, he felt the need to have a record of the dreams of a wealthy and prominent patient. He advertised for a stenotypist who could take dictation on the kind of machines that are used today only in law courts. The person he hired, Clara Marcus, remained with him from that time on as an assistant, editor, and his wife in the last five or six years of his life.

Dorothy Nyswander, Margaret Nyswander Manson, and Claudia Parsons all expressed the belief that Stewart's involvement with Marcus was a significant turning point in his work. As a highly organized and business-oriented person, she brought some degree of discipline to his life and handled the administrative and financial details of his group practice. In addition to taking down what was said in many of the therapy sessions, she also served as a typist and editor on the manuscripts he dictated to her. As Parsons put it in a letter to me of July 30, 1983: "She made herself indispensable to him both as housewife and amanuensis and indeed it needed someone with her purpose and drive to tidy up his life."

No sooner was Stewart settled into his private practice in New York than his plans were once again changed by the war. In July 1942, at the age of forty, he was drafted into the army. He was assigned to a special intelligence unit because Omer, serving as a lieutenant in an intelligence training unit, suggested to his superiors that Stewart might make a good interrogator because of his abilities as a hypnotist. But things did not work out for Stewart as a soldier, for the army had no use for his skills. He received a discharge in March 1943 and returned to private practice in New York until the war ended.[39]

But the interlude in the army turned out to be a provident one because it qualified Stewart for the GI bill and thus enabled him to move back to London as a student in 1946. After retrieving his data from Parsons, he registered once again for a Ph.D. at the London School of Economics. Since the London School at that time did not require any course work for the doctorate, he focused his attention on his dissertation.

Stewart and Marcus spent two years in London, Stewart dictating what Marcus told me were usually "page-long sentences," and Marcus editing and rewriting. His thesis advisers were two prominent anthropologists of the day, Raymond Firth and S. F. Nadel. According to Marcus, these advisers made Stewart rewrite the dissertation several times, much to her great annoyance.[40]

The final result of Stewart's stay in London was a 545-page dissertation entitled "Magico-Religious Beliefs and Practices in Primitive Society—A Sociological Interpretation of Their Therapeutic Aspects." Its primary theoretical focus is on the way in which the Senoi use of dreams and healing ceremonies is superior to the practices of Yami and Negritos, thereby allowing the Senoi a more open and creative psychological development. It also includes dozens of pages of purely descriptive material on the everyday lives of Yami and Negritos. More important for our purposes here, there are eighty-four pages of reported dreams in its appendices—312 from the Senoi, 192 from Negritos, and 316 from Yami.

There is a great deal of material on the Senoi in the dissertation that is similar to what has been reported by Pat Noone and later observers. There is also the kind of material on dream teaching and dream councils that has not been corroborated by anthropologists who learned the language and spent considerable time living among the people. Still, the dissertation usually does not make the large claims that are contained in the later articles. The different parts of the psyche according to the Senoi are discussed in sober fashion, and the village councils are characterized as "interminable."[41] In talking about dream control, the emphasis is on the dreams of the adepts or shamans, not the people in general. It is only shaman dreams that are claimed to demonstrate the decline in fear and attack dreams: "We have shown, however, that in the dreams of the Senoi shaman, the dream response to this category of changes [that is, fear and attack dreams] also reverses the early childhood patterns, causing the dream image of the thing which has been used, disturbed, or destroyed to appear as a spirit guide and make a creative contribution."[42]

Although this seldom-read dissertation contains most of the basic ideas that are presented in Stewart's published articles, it is most interesting today for what it does not say and does not demonstrate. Most of all, it makes no mention of the Senoi encouraging their children to have pleasurable dreams. Indeed, the only sustained discussion of pleasurable dreams is at the end of a section on the dreams of children and early adolescents. Here Stewart notes that there seems to be a *decline* in pleasurable dreams by early adolescence. He then speculates on the possible causes:

Also, his pure gratification dreams such as flying and eating become less pleasurable. Apparently, the social dictum that it is selfish to enjoy things without sharing them with the group is affecting the child's pleasurable dreams adversely as his growing confidence in himself and in the power of authority affects his fear dreams favorably.[43]

Also missing from the dissertation is any account of how the dreams were collected in the three societies. This is a notable omission because there is reason to believe from other evidence that they were collected and recorded in different ways in the three cultures. Among the Yami, for example, the dreams were very often—if not always—collected under hypnosis, and a Japanese policeman served as the interpreter both for the induction of hypnosis by Stewart and the reporting of the dreams by the Yami subjects.[44] Among the Senoi, on the other hand, the dreams were collected directly by Noone, who spoke Temiar, and then dictated to Parsons.

Moreover, the Senoi dreams were collected in different ways from different age groups. Children's dreams were collected by asking parents what their children had dreamed about. The dreams of teenagers and young adults were collected by asking them to report recent dreams. In the case of the older men, still another procedure was used. They were asked to recall all those dreams that they believed to be significant in bringing them to the status of adept or shaman.[45]

As for the Negritos, most of the dreams seem to have been collected in English-speaking schools set up by Americans, who had, of course, taken control of the Philippines as a protectorate after the Spanish–American War. Seventy-five percent of the Negrito dreams are from adolescents and preadolescents, a far higher percentage than in the other two samples. There are references in the dream reports to horses, streets, the Catholic church, and being chased by "wild Negritos," all evidence of the acculturation of these subjects.[46]

Considering the different ways in which the dreams were collected among the different groups and within the Senoi settlement, there is reason to be cautious about any claims concerning the superiority of Senoi psychological adjustment and flexibility that are based on alleged differences in dream content. For example, there is no strong evidence that night dreams and hypnotic dreams can be equated; a few studies suggest that this can be the case with some subjects under the right conditions, but other studies lead to the conclusion that night dreams and hypnotic dreams are different.[47] This is not a very strong empirical basis for the even greater leap of comparing hypnotic dreams from one culture with night dreams from another. Nor is the retrospective recall of dreams by shamans comparable to present-day recall by ordinary adolescents and young adults, or with parents' reports of what their children say they dream about.

These problems within the dissertation are serious enough to give pause, but the major problems with Stewart's claims about Senoi dream theory really began after he resumed private practice in New York and published his first article after completing the dissertation. "Dream Theory in Malaya" appeared in 1951 in *Complex,* a relatively new journal founded by author–critic Paul Goodman to explore the relationship between psychoanalysis and society. Although Stewart published three articles subsequent to this one, they make no major additions to the claims about the Senoi that he made at this time.

Stewart's published presentation of Senoi dream theory begins with a considerable inflation of his credentials. He calls himself an honorary fellow of the "Royal Anthropological Society" (*sic*) and a research fellow of "Peiping Union Medical College, Rockefeller Institute." In fact, the Royal Anthropological Institute elects only a handful of the most renowned anthropologists in the world as honorary fellows; Stewart was a regular fellow by reason of paying his dues.[48] Nor was Stewart a research fellow of the Rockefeller Institute. Although the exact nature of his few months of employment in Peking cannot be determined with final certainty, it seems most likely that he was paid out of the pocket of the psychiatric facility's wealthy American director.[49]

The paper also greatly exaggerates the amount of time Stewart spent studying the Senoi. The two or three months that he claims in his 1936 autobiography for the first trip (probably two to three weeks in reality) and the seven to eight weeks that Parsons documents for the second trip were said to be ten months in the dissertation. In the paper, the ten months become a year, and the two months in England with Noone become another year: "From a year's experience with these people working as a research psychologist, and another year with Noone in England integrating his seven years of anthropological research with my own findings, I am able to make the following formulations of the principles of Senoi psychology."[50]

After setting the stage by calling Senoi an "astonishing" people who are as advanced as if they came from another planet, Stewart states his most important assertion: "The Senoi believes that any human being, with the aid of his fellows, can outface, master, and actually utilize all beings and forces in the dream universe." To demonstrate this point, he uses the example of the falling dream. When children report a falling dream, he says, "the adult answers with enthusiasm, 'That is a wonderful dream, one of the best dreams a man can have. Where did you fall to, and what did you discover?'"[51] According to Stewart, the adult then says:

Everything you do in a dream has a purpose, beyond your understanding while you are asleep. You must relax and enjoy yourself when you fall in a dream. Falling is the quickest way to get in contact with the powers of the spirit world, the powers laid open to you through your dreams.[52]

Stewart then asserts that these instructions to the child bring about changes in the dreams. His authority for this claim is that he "made a collection of the dreams of younger and older Senoi children, adolescents, and adults, and compared them with similar collections made in other societies where they had different social attitudes toward the dream and different methods of dream interpretation." In the case of falling dreams specifically, the results are termed "astonishing":

The astonishing thing is that over a period of time, with this type of social interaction, praise, or criticism, imperatives, and advice, the dream which starts out with fear of falling changes into the joy of flying. This happens to *everyone* in the Senoi society.[53] [my emphasis]

Beyond the already mentioned difficulties of comparing the three different sets of dreams, the really astonishing fact is that the Senoi dreams in the dissertation do not provide any evidence whatsoever for these large claims. There are only four dreams in the 228 young-adult and adult dreams that might be interpreted as flying dreams, and they do not reveal any pleasure in flying or any ability to confront and conquer danger. Three are near-disasters. For example, one adult male had the following flying dream:

I dreamed that whilst out walking I came up to a house, not realizing that the mistress of the house was at home. But when I reached the ladder of the house, a woman appeared. Pulling me up by the hair, she urged me to go up with her. Not wishing to go up, I argued with the woman from below. Next moment, back came the woman's husband, and began to drive me away. When I could run no further, I began to fly through the air. Then I woke up.[54]

The only positive dream that mentions flying is a preshamanistic dream told in retrospect by an adult male. The flying occurs in passing in the context of a command from a potentially friendly spirit:

"Go and see your noose-trap [said the spirit]. If there is nothing, then I am deceiving you. If it is true, then you will know." Then he gave this command, "Cut tamu leaves to flourish in the *Jinjang*" [one of the dances at a song ceremony]. Then I joined in the *Jinjang* and sang until a dog barked "kerkus." I flew to Mount Gaet and stayed there five days. After staying five days, I plucked flower blossoms on the hill.[55]

There are four dreams in which falling occurs, three from young adult males, one from an adult male. None of them turns into a flying dream. A person falls to the earth and dies in two of the dreams, and a dreamer's "spirit" falls into the river and drowns in a third. In the fourth dream the dreamer fell from a tree into a marsh and "awoke with a start."[56] One of the dreams with a falling death has a happy ending, however. The spirit who had ordered the dead child to climb the tree in the first place brings it back to life.

The idea that pleasurable dreams should be pursued to a conclusion is introduced for the first time in this paper:

According to the Senoi, pleasurable dreams, such as of flying or sexual love, should be continued until they arrive at a resolution which, on awakening, leaves one with something of beauty or use to the group.

Dreams of sexual love should always move through orgasm, and the dreamer should then demand from his dream lover the poem, the song, the dance, the useful knowledge which will express the beauty of his spiritual lover to the group. If this is done, no dream man or woman can take the love which belongs to human beings.[57]

This general claim about pleasurable dreams contrasts greatly with the earlier-cited assertion in the dissertation that the number of pleasurable dreams seems to decline along about adolescence. Moreover, the discussion of sexual dreams in the dissertation makes no mention of this principle. Nor are there any sexual dreams in the collection that support the notion that the principle has any influence.

The relatively few dreams that even hint at sex, nine in all, are primarily what Stewart calls in the dissertation "sexual frustration dreams." Anger or fear is mentioned in five of them, and in only one is there any suggestion of pleasure. After reproducing four of the frustration dreams from younger adults in the main text, Stewart comments: "Such dreams of sexual frustration do not completely cease with adolescence, but we were told they rarely occur in the lives of the practising shaman."[58] But there are no data to back this up.

The several differences between the dissertation and the first published paper, and the lack of dream evidence in the dissertation for some of the claims in the paper, are important clues concerning the origins of Senoi dream theory. They are concrete evidence that Stewart's enthusiasm for his theories got away from him in his later discussions of the Senoi. This leads to the conclusion that the dream theory Stewart attributed to the Senoi in his published articles was in fact a creative amalgamation of his own ideas with what he had learned from his studies of hypnotic dreams, trance reveries, and night dreams among Yami, Negritos, Senoi, and his patients.

Parsons's account of Stewart, his 1936 autobiography, and my interviews and correspondence with people who knew him well make it clear that Stewart was not the kind of person who learned foreign languages and immersed himself in detailed studies of the cultures he visited. Instead, he was a wide-ranging thinker who let his imagination have free reign as he sifted through his experiences and what he was told by interpreters about his discussions with a few individual informants. Much of what he says in his dissertation about Senoi—or Yami, for that matter—is in agreement with what others have reported, but some of what he published is highly exaggerated or a starting point for what are actually his own ideas.

I believe Stewart was first and foremost a storyteller and healer in relating to the world. His participation in healing ceremonies and tribal dances had impressed him with the importance of magic rituals and joyful ceremonies in human life. He thought that modern life lacked social occasions of deep psychological significance. He kept repeating the fact that Westernized human beings had cut themselves off from the emotional and psychological wisdom of the nonviolent tribes he had studied and that the result was violence and homicide, mental disorders and war.

Indeed, Stewart's primary preoccupation in every one of his published articles—from the 1937 article on the Yami to a 1943 article, "Education and Split Personalities," to a 1962 article, "The Dream Comes of Age"—concerned the major social problems that faced the civilized world. He criticized the lack of cooperativeness and the indifference to equality in the 1937 article, the split personalities brought about by overly rationalistic educational systems in his 1943 article, the failure of scientists to study peace when "the engines of war today are terrifying" in a 1954 article, and the need to promote mental health and world peace through dream education in his 1962 finale.[59] These are not the usual concerns of a dream researcher.

In short, Stewart thought he had found the answers to modern societal problems in the ritual practices of primitive peoples. He thought the wisdom of tribal healers could be applied to today's world. Preliterate people, and especially the Senoi in his later years, had the answers to the problems of violence, insanity, and war. His desire to be a great healer and prophet led him to imbue his dream principles with the mystique of the nonviolent and easygoing Senoi.

The links that Stewart developed between his humanistic Rankian philosophy, his ideas about dreams, and the Senoi are comprehensible in the context of his desire to infuse modern life with what he saw as the deeper wisdom of tribal peoples. However, the linkages are tenuous ones at best. It would be more accurate if his claims about the efficacy of dream sharing and dream control were to be identified as his own principles or hypotheses. If it was better-known dream theorists such as Freud, Jung, and Perls who first suggested it is possible to understand ourselves through interpreting or acting out our dreams, then it was Stewart, not the Senoi, who first proposed that we actually might be able to share and control our dreams for our own pleasure and development rather than merely letting them happen to us. He may have come to the ideas in part from discussions with dream adepts in Senoi settlements, but the ideas were in fact his. For all his foibles, there is a magic about Kilton Stewart that transcends Senoi dream theory.

4

The Appeal of Senoi Dream Theory

The Senoi do not practice the so-called Senoi dream theory. It was Kilton Stewart who developed the novel idea that societies can benefit from sharing their dreams and that they can shape them through three principles of mind control. This is as clear as such matters can be. But we are left with a further puzzling question. Why did the ideas of Kilton Stewart, in the guise of an ancient tribal practice, suddenly resonate with a new generation of psychologically minded young adults of college backgrounds so many years after Stewart first introduced them?

The answers to this question will require a brief excursion into the sociology of an idea. In the pages that follow, I will attempt to demonstrate the influence that "experts" and "anthropological findings" can have on the lives of highly educated and urbanized Americans who are trying to transcend or reject American beliefs and values, only to have those beliefs and values reappear in unexpected ways. The discussion will of necessity be somewhat historical precisely because Stewart's claims about Senoi dream theory did not catch on immediately.

Stewart's claims received very little attention during the first decade or so after they appeared. The only social scientist who took any notice of them was Calvin Hall in *The*

Meaning of Dreams (1953). Hall's summary of Stewart's article "Dream Theory in Malaya" (1951) focused on the way in
which the Senoi shared dreams to reduce social tension, an
idea that made sense to him because of the success of psycho-
analysts in using dreams with patients to gain personal insights. However, Hall made no mention of the principles of
dream control, which did not fit either his Freudian belief in
a timeless and unchangeable unconscious or his empirical
findings on the consistency of individual dream patterns.

The larger response to Stewart's ideas, which came in the
sixties, was based on the dramatic social changes that
spawned the human potential movement as one of their
many consequences. For a brief moment, thanks to the civil
rights movement and the election of a charismatic young
president who promised to get the country moving again, it
seemed to be a time when all things were possible. The economy was good, colleges and universities were filling up with
the energetic youth of the baby-boom generation, the Peace
Corps provided an outlet for idealism, and America was going to the moon. The ideas of the humanistic psychologists
began to take hold, and people were experimenting with
LSD and other drugs that promised to expand the frontiers
of the human mind.

Senoi dream theory was one of the new possibilities that
captured the attention of those who were seeking to expand
human consciousness in the sixties. The idea that the sharing
of dreams could bring about greater social harmony and that
dreams could be shaped and changed through the application of the proper principles was attractive to social scientists
and psychotherapists of the new humanistic orientation.
Confront and conquer danger, go toward pleasure, extract a
gift from dream enemies—these ideas made sense to a generation that rejected "conservative" notions such as the unconscious for the idea of self-actualization. Senoi dream
theory was consistent with the interest in using meditation,

drugs, and other techniques to attain "altered states of consciousness."

Senoi dream theory entered the human potential movement by way of one of its major wellsprings, Esalen Institute near Big Sur, California, 165 miles south of San Francisco. As might be expected, the Senoi idea arrived at Esalen, probably in 1965, via a copy of Stewart's 1951 paper. Most of the people I talked with who were there at the time think that the paper was brought to the attention of Esalen leaders by Charles Tart, who was one of their friends and supporters. Tart, now a professor of psychology at the University of California, Davis, had a strong research interest in dreams, hypnosis, and parapsychology, and he recalls coming across Stewart's article in the early sixties in the course of his systematic search of all the past literature relating to dreams and altered states of consciousness. His personal experiences with the possibilities of dream control made the paper of immediate interest to him, but he is not sure whether it was he or one of his friends who actually brought the article to Esalen.[1]

Senoi dream theory was incorporated into Esalen planning for what was at first called the Experimental College and later the Residence Program. The idea was to go beyond weekend seminars and occasional visiting lecturers by developing a nine-month program that would gather together a diverse group of talented people under the tutelage of two full-time faculty members and a series of visiting experts. The fellows would experiment with a variety of consciousness-expanding techniques and then carry the best of them to colleges, professional associations, and other organizations around the country:

The curriculum would consist of meditation, encounter, sensory awareness, creativity, movement, emotional expression, inner imagery, dream work, and peak-experience training. There would be special sessions with the leaders who came to Big Sur to give seminars for the public; and there would be continuing work with the Esalen residents: sensory awakening with [Bernard] Gunther, gestalt therapy with Fritz [Perls] and Tai Chi sessions with Gia-fu [Feng] in the mornings. The prospective faculty was an eclectic group that included psychologists and artists and priests and even the Stanford track coach.[2]

These elaborate and ambitious plans were presented to the heads of large foundations in New York with the hope of obtaining major funding. The secretary of Health, Education, and Welfare in the Johnson administration, John Gardner, was contacted. However, neither the foundations nor Gardner would go beyond expressions of interest, and the size of the program had to be scaled down considerably. There would be only one faculty leader, Virginia Satir, a well-known family therapist, and no accompanying research program.

The new college of consciousness began in the fall of 1966 with seventeen resident fellows chosen from among about 200 applicants. They included an engineer; a Jesuit brother; a psychologist, Edward Maupin, who had done a dissertation on meditation at the University of Michigan; and a professor of art, Tom Allen, from Cabrillo Junior College in Santa Cruz, California. As it turned out, the program did not work out very well at all. Satir suddenly departed without warning or explanation after the first few weeks, and the fellows were left pretty much to their own devices. They floundered from experiment to experiment, including attempts to use Senoi principles of dream control, but none of the work was very conclusive. The program was somewhat more organized in its second year, but there was so much anxiety, conflict, and acting out within the group and among the program leaders that it was scaled down even more and then abandoned in the next few years.[3]

Although the Residence Program itself was a failure, a book that was based in part on some of its experiences was a great success. Entitled *Education and Ecstasy* (1968), it was written by George Leonard, a journalist and West Coast editor for *Look* magazine who had become very interested in the Esalen experiment and joined it as a director and adviser in 1965. Defining ecstasy in terms of delight and wonderment, Leonard called for a more emotionally based approach to the education of children that drew some of its inspiration from the human potential movement. At the same time, it also built on suggestions put forth by the behaviorist psychologist B. F. Skinner, who was as interested in the control of behavior as Stewart was in the control of dreams. He had written a utopian novel, *Walden Two,* in 1948 to show how "operant conditioning" based on "schedules of positive reinforcement" could create a better society. Leonard's book was serialized in *Look* just before its publication in 1968 and sold over 250,000 copies in its first few years.[4]

Stewart's claims about Senoi dream practices were introduced by Leonard in a futuristic chapter as one of the "Discovery Tents" at a school in the year 2001. The school was named Kennedy School, no doubt to capture the magic of the name that had rekindled hope for the young at the national level at the start of the sixties. The section on the Senoi explained the principles in Stewart's 1951 article and suggested that in the future every American child would learn them—along with biofeedback, body awareness, and other new psychological techniques that were just then appearing on the horizon.

Two chapters later, Leonard revealed to his readers for the first time that everything he had proposed as the fourth aspect of a new approach to education was being tried at a place called Esalen Institute. After noting that Esalen had been described by one of the founders of humanistic psychology, Abraham Maslow, as "probably the most important educational institute in the world," Leonard then explained that the institute was founded in 1961 and was named after the

tribe of Indians who had lived in that area.[5] He reported that
its founder, Michael Murphy, whose family owned the Esalen land, had spent nine years in "ascetic study and contem-
plation in the Eastern disciplines"; this included eighteen
months during which he meditated for six to eight hours a
day in an ashram in India. Murphy then "came back to his
native California convinced that the human potential, even
in the realm called 'mystical,' can best be achieved on an
American model, through an affirmation of the sensory universe." Murphy and Esalen were said to be at the cutting
edge of the human potential movement, and the new ideas
were being spread through seminars, workshops, and a
graduate-level Residence Program. The Senoi methods were
part of the program, which certainly sounded organized and
successful:

A residential program was initiated in September 1966, in
which graduate-level fellows spend nine months as full-time
free learners in the new domain. They practice meditation,
intensified inner imagery, basic encounter, sensory awareness, expressive physical movement and creative symbolic
behavior. They learn to control their brain-wave patterns,
using the simple brain-wave feedback device developed by
Dr. Joe Kamiya at the University of California Medical Center. They do extensive dream work, with the Senoi methods
described in the school of the future. They also practice the
all-action, anti-analytical Gestalt Therapy developed by the
venerable Fritz Perls, in residence at the Institute.[6]

Thus, Esalen and *Education and Ecstasy* were the starting
points in bringing Senoi dream theory into the mainstream
of the human potential movement and to the attention of the
general public. However, the avenue for bringing the ideas to
a wide audience of psychologists and their students was the
publication of Stewart's 1951 article in Tart's collection of
readings, *Altered States of Consciousness* (1969), which sold
over 50,000 copies in its first four years. Tart began his com-

ments on the Senoi: "You can imagine my amazement when I read that a whole tribe of primitive people, the Senoi of Malaya, had been practicing dream control techniques for centuries."[7] His amazement did not keep him from registering appropriate scholarly caution, noting that he had not been able to find corroborating accounts and that further research was needed. But his caution went unheeded. Instead, Tart's book gave further legitimacy to Stewart's claims. The psychologists who started Senoi dream groups in the late sixties and early seventies often traced their work to a reading of Stewart's article in Tart's book.[8]

Although the original interest in Senoi dream theory arose as part of the optimism and enthusiasm of the early sixties, a second push came, strangely enough, from the growing frustration and anger over America's widening involvement in the war in Southeast Asia. As young people turned against the war and the society that had produced it, they found great appeal in the fact that this new way of dreaming was not American. Instead, it was the practice of a nonviolent people who lived simply in another part of Southeast Asia and who were in many ways the opposite of Americans in their attitudes toward confrontation, aggression, and group violence. It was at this point that Stewart's own moral fervor about the social possibilities for Senoi dream theory resonated with the needs of his readers.

As the war continued and broadened despite massive demonstrations and other forms of protest, the daily newspaper and television revelations concerning its horrors also grew apace. Soon there was a growing rejection of anything connected with what was said to be an overly urbanized, industrialized, routinized, and intellectualized Western civilization. A mystique of the simple and the primitive gradually took hold. The Senoi were one small part of this mystique that included a glorification of Native Americans and their beliefs, especially their beliefs about dreams, visions, and

healing, as popularized most successfully in Carlos Castenada's alleged (but totally fabricated) conversations with a Ya-
qui Indian sorcerer, Don Juan.[9]

This rejectionist mood is best captured in Theodore Roszak's widely read and discussed book, *Where the Wasteland
Ends* (1972), which uses Senoi dream theory to bolster its
anti-Western critique. Roszak calls the environment of
urban-industrial civilization "artificial" and "inhuman."[10]
Even such sympathetic humanists as Buckminster Fuller
and Jacob Bronowski come in for criticism, Fuller for being
too fascinated with technological gimmicks, Bronowski for
an allegedly elitist attitude toward the wisdom of tribal cultures. Scientists and Bible-quoting fundamentalists are
lumped together as essentially similar because they both
concentrate on an objective, factual world.

No stone is left unturned in Roszak's relentless rejection of
the main currents of Western civilization, including the way
we sleep and awaken, and it is here that Stewart and Senoi
dream theory make their appearance. Americans see sleep as
a dead loss of time, says Roszak. They awaken too quickly
and immediately turn their attention to what they have to do
that day. They do not take their dreams seriously. They have
a "single vision" or tunnel vision.

This allegedly superficial attitude toward sleep and dreams
is then contrasted with what Roszak believes to be the superior wisdom of primitive cultures, and the Senoi are one of his
primary examples:

In some primitive cultures, like that of the Senoi of Malaya,
dream exploration is a highly sophisticated skill and a form
of pedagogy; indeed, Senoi oneirics makes our own poor
psychology of dreams seem sadly immature by comparison.
For the American Plains Indians, the more impressive dream
visions of a gifted medicine man like the Sioux Black Elk
could become the occasion for magnificent tribal ceremoni-
als in which the dream was re-enacted in careful detail, a

striking anticipation of what the Gestalt psychotherapist
Frederick Perls has, in our own time, recreated as "existential
dream interpretation."[11]

It was in this atmosphere that two popular books on
dreams appeared in 1974, which completed the mystification
of the Senoi. The first, by the British psychologist Ann Faraday, was *The Dream Game,* a "how-to-do-it" sequel to her
1972 best-seller, *Dream Power.* Whereas *Dream Power* had de-
voted only a few paragraphs to Stewart and his ideas, *The
Dream Game* spent several pages on Senoi dreaming and gave
every indication that the ideas worked.[12]

The second, Patricia Garfield's *Creative Dreaming,* was
even more crucial. Not only did it sell just as widely as Faraday's, but Garfield apparently provided independent evidence from her own discussions with the Senoi that Stewart
was correct about them. Moreover, Garfield reported that
she had talked with people in Singapore who were experts on
the Senoi. In short, Garfield's work was the clincher in creat-
ing the Senoi mystique because it provided the corroboration
that was needed before the skeptics could be convinced. She
seemed to be that necessary second opinion.

Yet Garfield's discovery of the Senoi and their dream theory was even more coincidental and happenstance than it
had been for Stewart. As she tells the story in the foreword
to her book, she was in Tokyo for the 1972 meeting of the
International Congress of Psychology. She mentioned to
Joe Kamiya, a pioneer dream researcher and discoverer of
biofeedback techniques, that she was going to visit Malaysia on the return trip. "If you're going to Malaysia, why not
visit the Senoi?" Kamiya asked casually. "The *who*?" replied Garfield.[13]

Kamiya then told Garfield about Stewart's ideas concerning Senoi dream practices, based on his reading of Stewart's
article in Tart's book. Garfield was intrigued enough to visit

the area for a day or two, but she never came close to a Senoi settlement. Instead, she talked to a few Senoi who were employed at an aboriginal hospital many miles from the jungle. She then reports: "I have studied Senoi dream practices by personally interviewing some members of the tribe (in English translated to Malay to Senoi who spoke both their aboriginal language and Malay)." But she also acknowledges a debt to Stewart, whom she read after she came home. She describes him as an "American trained in both anthropology and psychoanalysis who spent several years in Malaysia observing the Senoi use of dreams with Herbert [Pat] Noone, the British anthropologist, who gathered the basic data on these people."[14]

By 1974, then, the new myth was fully developed, and it was still going strong when I began my Senoi research late in 1982. Doubts were raised in 1978 when two documentary filmmakers came back from Senoi country with the news that they could find no morning dream clinics.[15] However, it was not until word of my findings and those of Dentan, Faraday, and Wren-Lewis began to get around, primarily through the *Dream Network Bulletin,* that the practitioners of the new dreamwork began to downplay the Senoi. Only in 1984, for example, did the Jungian-Senoi Institute change its name to the Jungian Dreamwork Institute.

To this point I have explained the appeal of Stewart's writings about the Senoi in terms of three factors: the legitimacy given to them by dream experts, the currency and publicity given to them by the human potential movement that grew out of the optimism of the early sixties, and the rejection of American society for a mystique of the primitive in the context of the antiwar movement. But this explanation is not complete. An emphasis on social change explains why people were open to new ideas in many areas of their lives, but it does not tell us why these particular ideas, and not others, were so readily accepted.

Paradoxical as it may sound, I think that Senoi dream theory had a deep appeal for Americans at this time because it was a new application of our deepest and most ingrained beliefs about human nature presented in the context of an allegorical story about community and authenticity. Very simply, the "Senoi way of dreaming" actually rests on the unquestioned American belief in the possibility of shaping and controlling both the environment and human nature. For Americans, but not for most people, and certainly not for the Senoi, human nature is malleable and perfectible. We are what we make ourselves. We can do it if we try. Senoi dream theory is an extension of that basic precept to the world of dreams. The fact that it is unwittingly presented in a mystique of the primitive only makes it all the more attractive. It is independent evidence for our convictions.

Perhaps the best-known American psychologist of the past forty-five years has been the behaviorist B. F. Skinner, whose ideas on education were incorporated into Leonard's *Education and Ecstasy*. Considering Skinner's general popularity and the near-fanatical loyalty of his followers, one should not be surprised that Skinner believes that all human behavior can be shaped and controlled through schedules of positive and negative (but preferably positive) reinforcement that are administered by agents of society. In terms of American psychology, then, Stewart is the B. F. Skinner of dreams, with his article "Dream Theory in Malaya" fulfilling the utopian function among his followers that *Walden Two* does among Skinner's. It was Stewart's achievement to apply the same American beliefs that give Skinner's behaviorism its inherent appeal to the seemingly uncontrollable happenings called dreams. Just as Skinner believed that behavior could be controlled with tangible rewards, so Stewart believed that dreams could be controlled with the social approval of group leaders.

However, too much credit for the application of these basic American assumptions should not be given to either of

these pioneers. American beliefs about the malleability of
human nature received practical implementation long before
psychologists happened on the scene. As several historians,
sociologists, and psychologists have shown, Americans have
embraced various techniques for self-control and mind control for many centuries. These techniques have ranged from
Benjamin Franklin's system of self-betterment through
"moral bookkeeping" (just write down the traits you want
to improve and then work on one each week, keeping track
of how you are doing), to the French psychotherapist Emile
Coué's repeated phrase "Day by day, in every way, I am getting better and better," to Norman Vincent Peale's "power of
positive thinking." We have made best-sellers out of self-help
books since very early in the nineteenth century, and we have
gone through numerous spiritual movements and mind-
control fads at crisis points in our history that are largely unknown to those who think that the surge of interest in such
techniques and formulas in the sixties was a new phenomenon. The only thing that seems to have altered is that these
ideas now are often placed within a psychological and therapeutic framework rather than a religious one.[16]

Viewed in this way, Senoi dream theory is typical American can-do. Taking hold in the sixties it was part of an attempt to conquer "inner space" at the very time that "outer
space" was being conquered by another set of new pioneers.
Indeed, the analogy between the conquest of "inner space"
and "outer space" was often made in the human potential
movement, just as Stewart had done in the opening paragraphs of his 1951 article.

But the ethnographies that appeal to us the most usually
contain more subtle messages than our most basic assumptions about human nature, and the story of the Senoi and
their dream theory is probably no exception. As James Clifford has argued in an attempt to understand the appeal of
these accounts at a deeper level, they are at least in part alle-

gorical stories that address fundamental issues about our own society or our own times.[17] When the well-known British anthropologist Edward Evans-Pritchard writes that the Nuer, a tribal people in Africa, are not caught up in time schedules and time pressures as we know them and then adds that "Nuer are fortunate," we begin to realize that we are being treated to nostalgic commentary about an imagined lost past as well as an account of another culture.[18] When Margaret Mead writes that young women come of age in Samoa with less tension than their American counterparts and then asks, in the final sentence of her classic book, "Will we, who have the knowledge of many ways, leave our children free to choose among them?" we know we have read an allegorical story about the way in which a liberal and pluralistic American society might deal with the breakdown of traditional family patterns, as well as a sensitive account of some aspects of Samoan adolescence.[19] Nor does Mead try to hide this level of her presentation. "Throughout her book," writes Clifford, "Mead presents the Samoan case as a lesson in human possibility for a troubled society."[20]

More generally, any ethnography runs the risk of being caught up in a search for origins, the lost past, or new alternatives. Building on earlier commentators, Clifford argues that most, if not all, studies of tribal cultures are underpinned by a "critical nostalgia" that is trying to determine how and where Western civilization supposedly went wrong. There is a search for "authenticity" that "presupposes and is produced by a present circumstance of felt inauthenticity."[21]

From this vantage point, Stewart's writings on the Senoi are at least in part an allegory about the search for community and a lost authenticity, and this also gave them a special appeal in the sixties. Certainly Stewart did not hesitate to draw such lessons throughout his writings. His work may differ from other ethnographic accounts in the scope and accuracy of its description of Senoi culture, but not in its underlying assumptions and the nature of its appeal. In many ways Senoi dream theory was a tale that fit the times, just as it was a story for all seasons in others.

But let us make no mistake about it. Such an analysis does not take away from the ideas or the spirit of the sixties. The interest in Senoi dream theory that developed then was a symbol of all that is best in the American character. It was one small flowering of what will come to be seen as one of the greatest decades in American history. It was a time when basic American values of individual freedom, equal opportunity, and civil rights began to be realized by more and more Americans through their own efforts—blacks, women, homosexuals, and the handicapped. It was a time when the young were able to express themselves in increasing numbers, and sexuality, mental illness, and abortion were able to come out of the closet. It was a time when creativity flourished in music and the arts at the grass-roots level, new ideas entered into university life, and the economy surged ahead on a wave of tax cuts, consumer spending, and the expansion of the welfare state—all this before and in spite of a bitter war relentlessly and arrogantly pushed forward by the best and the brightest of the American power elite, a war that drove millions of people into rebellion and the economy into inflation.

There were problems, too, of course, whether they be drugs, racists, maharishis, reactionary politicians, or people who helped to ruin the New Left because they thought a revolution was right around the corner, but the pluses far outweighed the minuses. It was an exhilarating time to be alive, and for some people believing in Senoi dream theory was one small part of it.

5

The Efficacy of Senoi Dream Theory

The fact that Stewart's theories of dream sharing and dream control are not practiced by the Senoi or that they were embraced rather uncritically by an eager new generation of ever-hopeful Americans does not invalidate his ideas. It may be that sharing dreams is beneficial for individuals, groups, or societies. It may be that Stewart's principles of dream control are useful in ridding dream life of the aggression and negative feelings that predominate over friendliness and positive feelings, as has been found in dreams from all over the world that have been studied systematically by Hall and others.[1]

The ideas put forth by Stewart are worthy of investigation whatever their origins or appeal. Even those who feel that my anthropological, biographical, and sociological analyses raise serious questions ought to concede that we owe it to these ideas to give them a fair hearing on the evidence. Thus, in this chapter I will assess the independent evidence that is available on the efficacy of sharing and shaping dreams. This evidence comes from classrooms, dream groups, experimental studies, and other tribal societies. The emphasis will be on systematic evidence whenever it is available, but I will report anecdotal information as well. I also suggest future studies of these issues where it seems relevant to do so and describe the limitations of experimental studies on such a theory.

There is not much systematic evidence on the usefulness
of dream sharing, but the little that exists is fascinating and
encouraging. In particular, the idea that the sharing of
dreams can lead to creativity and social harmony in small
groups received support in a classroom exercise carried out
over a period of several months in 1961 by Elena Goldstein
Werlin. Based in part on her knowledge of Stewart's work,
but also drawing on her reading of such experts on creativity
as Lawrence Kubie and Suzanne Langer, Werlin spontane-
ously asked her students early in the school year if they
would like to share their dreams:

The children were all sitting at their desks waiting for me to
tell them what the next activity would be when suddenly it
came to me, in a playful-serious way, "What about asking
them if they would like to tell their dreams?" Originally I
had been planning to have them draw, or listen to a story. But
then my old conviction about the value of telling dreams began bubbling and before I knew it I was asking the children if
they would like to tell a dream. I think at that moment my
curiosity about the validity of my readings concerning the
preconscious and creativity just got the better of me.[2]

Werlin then kept a classroom log over a six-month period,
in which she reports on the effects of dream sharing among
twenty-five first-grade children. Although there was "no
wild enthusiasm" for the idea of "dream time" in the first
few weeks, the children were often eager for these sessions
after a few months, and many sessions seemed to result in
reduced tensions in the classroom or heightened creativity
for some individuals.[3] However, it was not only dreams that
were shared, but as often daydreams or made-up stories.
Nor was any attempt made to interpret the dreams. Richard
Jones, the editor of the volume in which Werlin's account appears, comments in a footnote:

The surest way to discourage children from sharing their
dreams is to interpret them. Beginning teachers, interested

in psychology, must be reminded of this repeatedly. Dream interpretation is something one never finds children engaging in on their own. They seem to sense, if it ever occurs to them, that interpreting a dream is the least interesting thing that can be done with it.[4]

Instead, the dreams were seen only as a means of communicating or a basis for stories or drawings. For these purposes the children often related to the dreams they told and heard in a very constructive way. At the same time, Werlin felt that she gained an awareness of aspects of the children's personalities that she would not have been aware of if she had not instituted dream sharing:

During all times of the day except dream time Brenda and Robin and Patty pull in their feelers and become nearly completely withdrawn. But even if these quiet children are reticent for the rest of the day, the fact remains that they have participated in dream time and as a result a feeling of warmth and familiarity is able to grow between us.[5]

There are no comparable reports on the effects of dream sharing among older students, adults, or therapeutic groups. Many such groups have existed, but they go unreported or are discussed in a brief fashion with a very few examples. One of the few published reports in the journal literature, by Eric Greenleaf, provides three dreams that were elaborated or completed by dream groups. This 1973 article begins with the following introductory comment:

For the past three years I have conducted classroom and therapeutic groups based on a combination of these principles. Here I will discuss the organization of work in such groups and some instances of successful use of dream materials in effecting personal change and group cohesiveness.[6]

Although the Werlin and Greenleaf accounts are hardly enough in themselves to support the idea that dream sharing can be useful, the notion receives further support from the social psychology literature on sensitivity groups. The general conclusion that can be drawn from a wide range of such studies is that any personal disclosure in an open and supportive atmosphere is found by participants to be personally helpful and conducive to group cohesiveness.[7] Viewed in this way, dream sharing is useful because it is one of many intimate sharings that can have positive effects.

Even here, however, there is need for caution. It may be that people feel enthusiastic about sensitivity groups, therapy groups, and dream groups even when there is no objective evidence that anybody or anything changed. As psychologist Bernie Zilbergeld suggests on the basis of a detailed survey of the literature on psychotherapy and of his own interviews with therapists and former patients, there is a strong tendency to emphasize the positive and ignore the negative even when the group or individual therapy has not reached its stated goals. People are pleased to find they have been able to say personal or shocking things without being censured; they are glad to know they are not alone in their problems; and they have a strong will to believe that they must have gotten something out of an experience on which they spent much money and effort. Then, too, therapists and group leaders also have a way of claiming that the responsibility for success or failure lies with the patient, so people are reluctant to admit to negative outcomes.[8]

Still, it seems that dream sharing could be a somewhat unique kind of sharing because a dream is at once so personal and yet not seen as something for which the person is responsible. In some languages people say "It dreamed to me," and English speakers in effect express the same distance when they say things like "I had this dream." Greenleaf puts the contrast as follows:

What puzzles is that dreams, unlike other intimate communications, are unlikely to meet with criticism, ridicule or shocked surprise when told to strangers. Members of a dream group would no sooner call another's dream foolish than they would say having brown eyes was foolish. There is that "givenness" about dream material.[9]

Jones, in his comments on how dream sharing aided classroom communication in Werlin's study, makes a similar point in the context of Freud's theory that the mechanisms of the dream work produce an acceptable manifest dream out of latent wishes or thoughts:

As vehicles of communication, especially communication of the touchy sort, dreams serve admirably, as these two examples show. Very likely this is due to the dream's being at once intrinsically playful, strategically removed from reality, uniquely candid in emotional import—and all this automatically so, having already been accomplished by the dream work.[10]

Whatever the reasons for the peculiar status that dreams enjoy as personal statements for which we are not responsible, it seems that further studies of their usefulness in groups could be conducted within the framework of intimacy and self-disclosure literature. These studies could directly compare dream sharing and other types of disclosures within experimental groups on the variety of dependent variables that are used in sensitivity studies, including individual ratings of others in the group and experimenter ratings of individual reactions and group interactions. Studies of this kind are not likely to determine whether or not dream sharing could lead to the larger, societywide harmony that Stewart hoped for, but they would be a starting point on the personal and social usefulness of this idea.

There has been relatively little work on the idea of shaping or controlling dreams, and only part of it was conducted with Stewart's claims in mind. As Charles Tart notes in a review of these studies: "The number of actual studies of control of the content of dreams is far too small to assess adequately the ef-

porate it, but only three of the eight who received the negative suggestion succeeded. (Four of the eight people who received no suggestion dreamed about eating anyway.)[17]

A still unpublished brief report to the 1977 meeting of the Association for the Psychophysiological Study of Sleep also showed some presleep influence on general dream content. Its authors tried to influence the dreams of twenty-four female subjects who strongly disliked snakes. Six of the subjects were instructed to have pleasant dreams involving a snake, six to have pleasant dreams about a neutral animal, six to have unpleasant dreams involving a snake, and six to have unpleasant dreams about a neutral animal. Subjects saw a live snake before going to sleep and upon awakening.

Dreams were collected through awakenings in the sleep laboratory. Those who were told to have pleasant dreams seemed to do so in terms of higher levels of happiness and friendliness and lower levels of anxiety, sadness, and aggression on dream content scales.[18] However, no information is provided on the magnitude of the effect or the number of subjects who were influenced. Nor is there any mention of whether or not those who were instructed to dream about snakes either positively or negatively actually did so. A letter to one of the co-authors failed to bring any further information. Until such time as a full account of the study is published, it can be considered as only suggestive.

These presleep suggestion studies are not direct evidence for Stewart's claims because their focus is on incorporation, not control. They do not speak to the question of whether or not typical dream content, such as falling or being chased, can be altered by suggestions or instructions. However, there is some direct evidence for the possibility that Stewart's principles might have some usefulness.

This comes from the personal testimony of two dream book authors, Ann Faraday and Patricia Garfield. Both report that they have altered their dream content by the use of his principles. In Garfield's case the claim is especially interesting because she had been keeping a dream journal long before she heard of Stewart's work. She reports that her use of Stewart's techniques led to both a decline in the number of dreams in which she was a helpless victim and an increase in the number of dreams in which she had orgasms.[19] However, no one had copies of her dreams before she started to use the control techniques, nor has any independent judge analyzed the dream series quantitatively.

Tart also reports that he can "attest to the validity of one aspect of Senoi dream technique through personal experience." However, he did not learn the technique from Stewart but hit upon it himself as a child:

I discovered this technique myself as a young child of about eight, when I was troubled by nightmares. Feeling that the nightmares were *my* dreams and so should be responsive to me instead of frightening, I taught myself to go back to sleep and into the dream as quickly as possible, and either conquer the frightening image or make friends with it. After fewer than a dozen dreams where I did this, nightmares became a very rare occurrence with me and my dreams took on a very positive, happy tone. I taught the technique to my son when he was having frightening dreams around age four, and it quickly worked for him.[20]

Beyond personal testimony, there is an unpublished dissertation from the University of Arizona in 1978 that examines dream control with some report of success. Entitled "Dream Control for Behavioral Change," it goes one step beyond the usual studies in attempting to determine whether or not dream control can lead to behavioral changes. Thirty-eight percent of twenty-one experimental subjects reported controlling one or more of their dreams. However, these subjects did not do any better than the others on the Subjective Anxiety Scale that was being used to measure behavioral consequences.[21] There is no indication in the psychological literature of any follow-up on this study.

There is only one published paper in the psychology research literature that reported any positive results on dream control through presleep efforts. Inspired at least in part by Stewart's writings, psychologist Rosalind Dymond Cartwright asked seventeen college subjects to list personal traits they would like to change and then urged them to have positive dreams about one of these traits. They were told to wish over and over again as they fell asleep for the change they wanted to make; for example, I wish I were not so hostile, I wish I were not so irritable, I wish I were more poised.

Fifteen of the seventeen subjects had at least one instance of apparent incorporation of the target trait when they were awakened in the laboratory to report dreams. However, eleven of the seventeen also showed instances of incorporating another desired trait that had not been wished for. Thus, the magnitude of the effect was not very large even though the results reached conventional levels of statistical significance.

But this result only refers to incorporation, not to control. In only two instances of incorporation did the content show the positive changes that were sought. Instead of having positive incorporations, more often than not the subjects incorporated the negative trait and seemed "to be getting some gratification out of maintaining it."[22] In the example Cartwright provides, a subject who wished to be less sarcastic had two different dreams in which she was very sarcastic. In other words, this study of dream shaping through a straightforward personal wish was not as successful as it first appears.

Another piece of seemingly positive evidence from Cartwright's laboratory turned out to be inconclusive. This second study first came to public attention as one that seemed likely to lead to positive results. In "Happy Endings for Our Dreams," which appeared in *Psychology Today* in 1978, Cartwright reported that she and her associates were attempting to alter the dream plots of sixty recently divorced women. Her comments on the ongoing study began by saying that some of the women "occasionally do succeed."[23] Beyond this preliminary report, however, no results from the second study were published. In reply to my request for further information, Cartwright wrote me in July 1983: "The dream control studies mentioned in the *Psychology Today* article never got beyond the pilot stage as NIMH [National Institute of Mental Health] could not be convinced that they were doable."

Perhaps the most promising experimental evidence for the possible control of dreams comes from work on a phenomenon known as lucid dreaming. [Lucid dreaming means very simply that dreamers are aware that they are dreaming during the dream itself.] Although the frequency of lucid dreaming varies greatly among subjects, Tart estimates that as many as 10 percent of the population has experienced at least one lucid dream. He quotes a classic lucid dream by the Dutch physician Frederick van Eeden, who was among the first to discuss them in any detail:

On Sept. 9, 1904 I dreamt that I stood at a table before a window. On the table were different objects. I was perfectly aware that I was dreaming and I considered what sorts of experiments I could make. I began by trying to break glass, by beating it with a stone. Yet it would not break. Then I took a fine claret-glass from the table and struck it with my fist, with all my might, at the same time reflecting how dangerous it would be to do this in waking life; yet the glass remained whole. But lo! when I looked at it again after some time, it was broken.[24]

[The primary emphasis in lucid dreaming is upon an awareness or consciousness that is similar to what the person experiences while awake, but the idea of controlling content within the dream is a frequent subsidiary aspect. The control within a lucid dream, however, is developed within the dream itself, not through presleep training, as is thought to be the case in the Senoi method.]

The phenomenon of lucid dreaming has been remarked upon by several commentators over the past 100 years, but until recently it has not been studied in a systematic fashion. Tart notes in his review of the topic that "most of the sparse literature on lucid dreaming consists of self-reports by lucid dreamers, sometimes embedded in a literary matrix."[25]

Since 1979, however, the anecdotal and literary nature of the evidence on lucid dreams has been overcome to some extent in a series of studies that are in their preliminary phases and need to be repeated in other laboratories. In these studies lucid dreamers are instructed to communicate their lucidity through eye movements and fist clenches. One published study of this type claimed that five subjects were able to make signals in thirty of thirty-five lucid dreams that could be detected by independent judges studying the electrophysiological records made of the sleep periods.[26]

Some of these lucid dream studies are also concerned with dream control, but the first reports on this dimension are less encouraging than on the attainment of lucidity. In one such study, experienced lucid dreamers were instructed to turn on a light in the dream. Only two of sixteen subjects reported that they were successful.[27] Still, lucid dream studies are in their infancy, and experimental work with a variety of induction techniques may make it possible to increase the number of lucid dreamers and the degree of their dream control.[28]

The hypnotic studies, the presleep suggestion studies, the testimony by dream book authors such as Garfield and Faraday, and the studies on lucid dreaming—all provide some support for Stewart's ideas about dream control. In particular, the studies are of interest because they suggest that some dream control can be achieved within an experimental situation with very little training. They suggest the possibility that greater control might be achievable if people received a longer period of training in a supportive social context.

At the same time, there is also evidence that dreams cannot be controlled even to a small extent within dream groups or experimental situations. Two of the earliest leaders of Senoi dream groups, Joel Latner and Meredith Sabini, wrote as follows in an article that is very positive toward dream discussion groups as a way of heightening personal sensitivity and enhancing creativity:

We have had scant success with instructed dreaming, but we have harvested some fruits in them. One of us has awakened from a dream with artwork patterns which could be carried out in pastels, and the other has awakened with lines— words, or music, or both, for songs he was writing.[29]

Ironically, a strong piece of negative evidence comes from a 1974 study by Garfield. In this study a good dream recaller spent five months trying to increase the frequency with which his hands appeared in dreams. (Carlos Castenada claimed that his mythical sorcerer, Don Juan, often focused on his hands while dreaming.) The subject also spent twelve months trying to increase the frequency of flying dreams. But the frequency of hand images stayed the same and the frequency of flying dreams rose only from 2 to 4 percent. Garfield attempts to rescue these findings by claiming that some of the hand dreams became more vivid and some of the flying dreams included intense sensations, but the frequencies speak for themselves against these after-the-fact interpretations.[30]

Two very careful and detailed studies of dream control by psychologists David Foulkes and M. L. Griffin were also unable to report any positive results. In the first study, twenty-three subjects were taught the Stewart control techniques as described in Garfield's book and were asked to dream about a randomly assigned target that was selected from a list of six dream suggestions. The subjects kept daily records of the dreams they remembered over ten consecutive nights, and two independent judges attempted to match dreams with target suggestions. Their matchings did not exceed what would be expected by chance.[31]

The second study used twenty-nine highly motivated subjects who claimed some previous success in dream control or great interest in the topic. They too tried to dream about targets from a list of six dream suggestions. This time, however, the chosen targets were more carefully monitored by the experimenters "so as to be better equated for emotional tone, amount of detailed elaboration of content, and degree of specific personal relevance." This study also covered ten nights, but this time subjects were allowed to pick the nights on which they felt they were most likely to be able to control their dreams. The subjects reported an average of seven dreams. Four independent judges attempted to match these dreams to the target suggestions. Once again, the correct matches did not exceed what would be expected by chance. The authors reached the following conclusion:

These results cannot, of course, "disprove" the possibility of deliberate presleep dream control. They do indicate, however, that if such control is possible, it must be much more difficult to achieve than enthusiasts such as Garfield generally intimate.[32]

A similar lack of results was reported in a laboratory study by a team of Canadian researchers who assessed physiological reactions as well as dream content. In this study seven females and three males aged nineteen to twenty-nine were instructed to either increase or decrease their emotional involvement in their dreams on the fourth and sixth nights of seven consecutive nights in the sleep laboratory. There was a slight increase in the variability of heart rate and respiration on experimental nights, but dream content measures did not show the anticipated changes in emotionality. The authors concluded that their instructions induced stress, but no changes in the dreams.[33]

These negative reports, while not encouraging for the dream control hypothesis, are not without one important defect—from Stewart's standpoint. None of them provides a social context for the implementation of his principles. The experimenter merely suggests to the individual subjects, or tells them to suggest to themselves, that they dream about some personal trait or wished-for action. In Stewart's view, which shows a good instinct for findings in social psychology, these principles work only when they are imbedded in a group context and advocated by social authorities who are in some way or another trusted leaders or role models for those learning the principles. It is the group leaders who provide the social authority that allows participants to explore the idea that they can control their dreams. As Stewart summarized his view in 1962:

The analysis of the cross-cultural data proves that the individual cannot change, simplify, and reorganize the inwritten social patterns without the cooperation, permission, and assistance of inwritten social authorities. It not only requires the cooperation of the dream model of the dream interpreter in the dream to effect progressive reorganization; also, apparently this dream reorganization is largely confined to fulfilling the directives received from and agreements entered into with the dream interpreter while the dreamer was awake.

It is also necessary, in Stewart's view, to share and evaluate dreams in order to gain control of them:

Furthermore, the reorganizing effect of each individual dream appears to diminish and lose its validity as the foundation for a further step if the dream is not socially expressed, evaluated, and approved by a respected peer or authority.[34]

Thus, a more complete experimental test of Stewart's principles of dream control would include the following features. First, it would utilize subjects who have kept dream journals that are in the hands of the investigators before the study begins. Such subjects could be chosen from among the surprising number of people who record their dreams as part of a general diary, out of curiosity, or for use in literary or artistic projects. Second, subjects would be screened to assure that they are open to the possibility that dreams can be

shaped; at the same time, those who are already "true believers" would be excluded because the experimenters need to
be sure they are receiving accurate reports.

Third, while the subjects would not be true believers, at
least one of the investigators would be a strong believer in
order to create the proper atmosphere. Since, according to
Stewart, the basis of any dream control begins with the permissive suggestions of a respected social authority, it would
be important that the person teaching the principles be able
to convey his or her convictions to the subjects in a group
setting and to meet with the group in a supportive fashion to
discuss individual dreams during the time of the study.

Fourth, the dream content to be controlled would involve
material that frequently appears in dreams and relates to
the principles of control. It would be useful, for example, to
focus on changing the degree to which the dreamers are
victims in aggressive interactions or on increasing the
number of friendly interactions. Both are social interactions that relate directly to the principles of confronting
danger and moving toward pleasure. Moreover, they can be
scored reliably and compared with the general norms developed for American college students by Hall and Robert Van
de Castle.[35]

Fifth, whatever content is targeted for change, subjects
would write down or report their dreams each day for later
scoring by independent judges. Ideally, these judges would
not know anything about the nature of the study, but at the
least they would not know whether any given dream came
from before or after the experimental phase of the study began. The study could be designed for everyday recall in the
home setting, for awakenings in the sleep laboratory, or for a
combination of both.

But even such a study has significant limitations because it
lacks the important dimension of socialization within a cul-

turally supportive context. It may be that dream control could be achieved if it were taught to children from a young age. Recall, for example, that Tart reports he was able to pass on his self-discovered method of controlling nightmares to his four-year-old son with very good results.[36] There are also some instances in the anthropological literature where children appear to have been taught by their parents to allay anxiety in dreams, to have certain kinds of dreams, or to talk with or touch spirits in trance states.[37] These examples can be considered as no more than suggestive, but they make the point that there may be limitations to any experimental tests of what is best understood as a socialized cultural belief.

Whatever future experimental or anthropological studies may reveal, the conclusions that can be drawn about the efficacy of Senoi dream theory at this time are not very positive ones. Still, there may be a little more substance to the theory than readers may have expected. Whether the issue is dream sharing or dream shaping, there is at least some evidence, direct or indirect, anecdotal or systematic, that Stewart's ideas may have some usefulness. Until such time as more convincing studies are carried out, however, the weight of the evidence is such that his ideas cannot be advocated with any expectation of much success. As with many other dream ideas, Stewart's principles about dream sharing and dream control remain hopeful possibilities that rest largely upon the intuitions of a unique dream theorist and the reports of success by a few individuals.

While this may not appear to be a very satisfying conclusion to a chapter that has reviewed a wide range of research studies, it must be viewed within the context of my final chapter, in which I evaluate theories about other aspects of dreams and discuss the problems of attaining reliable knowledge about these uninvited visitors of the night.

6

The Mystery of Dreams

We can summarize the conclusions of the previous chapters as follows. The Senoi are indeed nice people, but they do not practice "Senoi dream theory" as we know it. Kilton Stewart was a well-meaning charmer and storyteller, but in his eagerness to be a prophet, he misunderstood the Senoi and incorrectly attributed his own ideas to them. Senoi dream theory seemed sensible to many Americans during the turbulent sixties, but that is because it combined a new application of traditional American ideas about the malleability of human nature with a story about a lost authenticity. And the evidence that dream sharing may be useful or dream control possible is only suggestive at this time.

But there are ways in which these conclusions are too stark and harsh. They need to be leavened by a consideration of the findings in other areas of dream research in order to see what has been gained by Stewart's claims about Senoi dream practices. More generally, the examples of confusions and misunderstandings are legion within every field of the social sciences. It seems to be the task of each new generation of social scientists to show that the claims of their elders are not as sound as had been thought, only to have the next generation realize that these critics had been equally misguided in ways they never would have guessed. We always forget to be skeptical about ideas whose time we wish would come, especially ideas that fit our deepest prejudices about human nature and society.

It will be the purpose of this concluding chapter to provide a more rounded assessment of the contribution that Kilton Stewart has made to our understanding of dreams. It will do so in the context of what we do and do not know about dreams in general and in the light of the basic problems of generating reliable knowledge on any issue concerning dreams. Only then will it be possible to see if our horizons have been expanded by this encounter with Senoi dream theory.

Why do we dream? That question has been debated since the dawn of Western civilization. It has been the object of scientific interest at least since Freud suggested that the "function" of dreams is to preserve sleep through the hallucinatory satisfaction of wishes. But beyond simple "dreams of convenience," such as drinking a glass of water or getting dressed for school, no convincing evidence outside of Freud's interpretative framework has been put forth that lends support to this view.[1] Numerous other theories have been proposed to explain why we dream—to assimilate anxiety, to master problems, to integrate new information, and, most recently, to get rid of redundant or useless memories.[2]

But there are no studies that substantiate or disprove any of these conjectures either. It has proved impossible so far to devise suitable studies of these ideas. Some researchers doubt that such studies will ever be undertaken because functionalist theories are, by their very nature, untestable. They explain everything and nothing within the context of the present-day scientific worldview. Perhaps this point was made most succinctly by the British cyberneticist W. Ross Ashby in *Design for a Brain* (1960): "Never explain an action in terms of its advantage or use—that is circular if one is an evolutionist."[3] Thus, in answer to the question, why do we dream, it is still as plausible to believe with the Senoi that dreams are the adventures of the soul at night as it is to believe that they are attempts to preserve sleep or to clear trivial information out of the brain's software components.

If we don't know why we dream, we also don't know much about why some people recall a great many dreams and other people remember hardly any. The usual belief, derived from Freud, in a line of reasoning with which he may or may not have agreed, is that people who don't recall their dreams tend to deny or repress them or are not open to their inner experiences. But there have been many studies trying to relate personality characteristics to dream recall, and the results are not very impressive. The findings are often contradictory, and any patterns that emerge are minor ones.[4]

Discouraged by these results, researchers turned to an exploration of factors other than personality that might affect recall, such as the person's motivation to recall, ability to develop visual imagery, and various kinds of memory abilities. These studies have had a little more success, but the results are still not very impressive. We now know that many non-recallers can be made into recallers if they can be motivated to have an interest in dreams and are taught such small tricks as jotting down notes when they awaken in the night or sitting in bed in a relaxed fashion when they awaken in the morning. We also know from several studies that memory tests seem to predict the ability to recall a little better than personality tests. But the new studies do not add up to a comprehensive answer. The best that can be said is that the traditional personality hypothesis is not as important as had been thought and that dreams are probably remembered or forgotten by different people for different reasons.[5]

Nor do we know when we dream. We probably dream during sleep, of course, but all the evidence that exists can be interpreted just as readily by the idea that we dream while we are waking up.[6] However, for a brief, euphoric time in the late fifties and early sixties, it was firmly believed that dreams occur only during a stage of sleep called a REM period, REM standing for the Rapid Eye Movements that are one of the most striking characteristics of this activated stage of sleep.

But that claim did not hold up. People awakened from the other stages of sleep, which are called non-REM periods, also remember dreams, not quite as often, but often enough to invalidate the strict REM-dream correlation that has become part of popular culture.[7] Indeed, the REM–dream equation is now so widely accepted in American society that it is worth exploring in some detail; the story of how this belief developed and then was disconfirmed in most of its particulars is evidence that dreams can be almost as elusive for hard-nosed laboratory scientists as they were for an American adventurer in the jungle.

Physiological work on dreams began accidentally in the early fifties in an old and respected sleep laboratory at the University of Chicago, where studies of sleep had been going on with little or no attention to dreams for almost thirty years. The new work began when a graduate student who was studying breathing during sleep in new-born babies noticed that there were two phases in infant sleep, a quiescent phase, in which nothing much seemed to be happening, and an active phase, in which there were body movements, respiration changes, and most of all, eye movements.[8] Students and professors at the laboratory soon confirmed that there were somewhat similar phases in adult sleep, complete with changes in brain wave patterns. The thought arose that the active phase of sleep might correlate with dreaming, and subsequent studies found that awakenings from REM periods led to 74 to 88 percent dream recall.[9] The few reports from non-REM awakenings were explained away as thought fragments or memories from earlier REM periods.

The claims of this research led to a renewed interest, within psychology, in dreams and dreaming. Indeed, dreams suddenly had a unique standing within psychology, for here was the first one-to-one relationship between a psychological experience and a physiological indicator such as brain wave patterns. The fact that the eye movements seemed to correspond with the action in the dream in some highly publicized instances added to the excitement.[10]

The media attention for the REM–dream connection was even greater than it was to be later for the Senoi. Between 1959 and 1962 there were major articles in such popular magazines as the *Saturday Evening Post, McCall's, Newsweek, Time, Popular Science, Science Digest, Today's Health,* and the *New York Times Magazine.* The articles had titles like "Dream and Stay Sane," "How Dreams Keep Us Sane," and "Science of Dreams."

Soon there appeared a highly readable book called *The Science of Dreams* (1962) by *Newsweek* science editor Edwin Diamond. The book grew out of an April 1959 cover story on dreams that he did for the magazine. Diamond interviewed all the principals, and he spent a night in a dream laboratory that included five awakenings to report dreams. His account is a serious one that accurately captures the mood of the people he interviewed. After telling about a typical awakening in the sleep laboratory, he announced the importance of the findings he was about to recount with no hesitation or uncertainty:

As a result of thousands of similar experiments conducted since 1952, centuries of speculation and popular mythology about dreams and sleep have at last been set straight. For the first time the amount, frequency, and content of dreaming have been precisely determined; we now know that dreaming is as natural as eating or breathing, that every night every one of us dreams every ninety minutes of sleep. The length of these dreams runs from ten minutes to almost one-half hour.[11]

The book reported the best examples researchers had to offer on how the eye movements correlated with the dream action. It told of stunning studies in which subjects deprived of their REM sleep became nervous and hallucinatory the next day. People deprived of REM time made it up as soon as they were allowed to sleep normally. "It is as though a pressure to dream builds up with the accruing dream deficit during successive dream-deprivation nights," one investigator reported.[12] A need to dream had been discovered.

But only some of these new claims turned out to be true. A great deal had been learned about sleep, but very little about dreams. The first cloud on the horizon appeared when dream researchers from other laboratories began to find that dream reports could be obtained from non-REM periods. The percentages on non-REM dream recall went from 7 to 27 percent and even 65 percent.[13] A study published in 1983 involving 160 awakenings found that 93 percent of REM awakenings and 67 percent of non-REM awakenings led to reports of some kind.[14] It became almost as logical to say that REM reports were memories from non-REM periods as to say that non-REM reports were leftovers from REM periods.

The claim that eye movements correlated with dream content also failed to withstand close scrutiny. A study based on dozens of awakenings during unusual eye movement patterns established that independent judges could not match eye movement patterns with dream reports. Even the experimenters themselves could not see any connection between eye movement patterns and dream reports when they had both protocols in front of them.[15]

Two further studies of this issue from yet another laboratory added further support to these negative findings. They showed that eye movement patterns are very similar from subject to subject and that the eye movements are very different from those in waking life. They also found some eye movements during non-REM sleep. In 18 percent of the REM awakenings in one of the studies, the eye movements were in the direction to be expected from the dream content, but in another 10 percent they were exactly the opposite. There was no semblance of a relationship in the other 72 percent of the awakenings.[16]

Other information on eye movements during sleep began to cast doubt on their relationship to dreams. Neonates and people without cortexes were found to have the same eye movement patterns as normal adults. Then, too, the patterns were found in every species of mammal as well as some birds and reptiles.[17]

Some researchers tried to save the REM–dream equation with the hypothesis that the "mentation" reported from REM periods was more "dreamlike" than the shorter, more abstract, and more thoughtlike reports that were said to come from non-REM periods. But several laboratories reported very quickly that the differences did not seem very great.[18] In one blind scoring of REM and non-REM reports for the elements that seem to characterize what we think of as "dreamlike," it was found that many non-REM reports were indistinguishable from REM reports.[19] Later studies showed that there were very few differences between REM and non-REM dream reports if the length of the reports was taken into account.[20] Although there may yet prove to be some differences in what is reported from the two different types of sleep, the similarities seem to far outweigh the differences at this time.

Nor could the "REM deprivation" studies showing dramatic effects from interfering with REM sleep be replicated with any regularity. In some studies, subjects showed the "rebound" effect of making up lost REM time when allowed to sleep normally, but they did not show any nervousness or other symptoms. Still other subjects were found who did not make up their lost REM time and yet did not become mildly neurotic during the day.[21] Moreover, it was found that subjects deprived of non-REM sleep often showed a pressure to make up lost non-REM time. And when subjects were totally sleep-deprived, they spent most of their sleep time in non-REM sleep when they were allowed to sleep.[22] A need to dream cannot be untangled from these various studies.

In spite of the disappointment that followed these negative findings, some new information had been gained about dreams from the hundreds of studies that were inspired by "the new biology of dreaming." For example, we now know that dreams can be recalled from any stage of sleep, although they seem to be better recalled from REM periods and from awakenings later in the sleep period. It has been affirmed that it is difficult or impossible to instigate dreams with external stimuli and that ongoing dreams are only affected in a minor way by such stimuli. It has been shown that dreams from early in the night do not differ from those later in the night in any systematic way and that dreams collected from awakenings throughout the night are basically similar to those remembered during the day aside from a certain blandness in their content.[23]

The difficulties of obtaining dreams from children aged three to five have been demonstrated, leading to the hypothesis that dreaming develops in parallel with the acquisition of language skills. Changes in dream content from the ages of five to fifteen have been discovered.[24] New information on dream recall has also been developed. If dreams recalled during three or four laboratory awakenings during the night are compared to the ones the person still remembers in the morning, the dreams recalled in the morning are the most recent, the longest, and the most dramatic, precisely the factors that would be predicted by classical memory experiments.[25]

Many other lesser findings about dreams from laboratory studies could be outlined here, but the more important point is that the early claims did establish a research tradition, even though these claims were seriously in error on many crucial points. The laboratories that were set up in response to the provocative findings of the first dream investigators were able to correct the mistakes and go on to other work. Thus, the greatest contribution of these laboratory studies was the new interest they kindled in studying dreams, a contribution that only slightly outweighs their inadvertent demonstration that dreams cannot be reduced to physiology.

Perhaps the most reliable and systematic information that exists on dreams concerns what people actually dream about. Since 1945 Calvin Hall and his co-workers have collected dreams from classrooms, clinics, tribal settings, and the dream diaries of both famous and ordinary people. Using an objective scoring system that allows the dream analyst to categorize and tabulate frequencies for such dream elements as settings, characters, objects, social interactions, good fortunes, misfortunes, and emotions, they have been able to demonstrate sex differences, age differences, cross-cultural similarities, and personality differences in dream content with a considerable degree of reliability.

For example, men usually dream much more about other men than they do about women. Their most typical interaction with these men is an aggressive one, especially if the men are strangers to the dreamer. On the other hand, interactions with women, who constitute one-third of the characters in men's dreams, are likely to be friendly ones. Women, by way of contrast, dream about equally of women and men, and they have roughly the same ratio of friendly and aggressive interactions with both sexes, even though male strangers present problems for them too. Moreover, there is less friendliness and aggression in their dreams than in men's, and the aggression is more likely to be verbal than physical.[26]

Van de Castle, Hall's major co-worker during the sixties, reports further sex differences in American subjects:

Women pay more attention to clothing and jewelry and focus upon descriptions of a person's face, hair, and eyes. Men express more interest in automobiles, tools, weapons, and money, while women are interested in household objects and flowers. There are more characters appearing in women's dreams and these are more likely to be single characters who are familiar, such as mothers, family members, children and babies. Groups of unfamiliar characters appear in men's dreams and men are more prone to identify others on the basis of their occupational status.[27]

These findings on American sex differences are based on 1,000 dream collected from 500 men and 500 women at Case Western Reserve University around 1950. Dreams collected in 1980 from fifty-three males and sixty-nine females at the University of Richmond provided the opportunity to see if anything had changed over the thirty-year period. Nothing much had. Among forty comparisons in a wide variety of content categories, there were only six statistically significant differences for male comparisons and three for female comparisons. For example, both males and females at the University of Richmond had a higher proportion of "known" or "familiar" characters and a lower proportion of friendly interactions than their Case Western forerunners. Most important for our purposes here, there were no changes in any of the sex differences that had been found earlier. This first "historical" study of dream content suggests that some things don't change, or only very slowly.[28]

Children's dreams differ in several ways from those of adults. There are many more animal characters in their dreams, for example, and most of the encounters with these animals are frightening or aggressive ones. Children are also much more likely than adults to be victims of aggression as opposed to initiators of aggression, and there are more misfortunes such as getting lost or becoming ill in their dreams.[29]

The repetitiveness of what individuals dream about is a persistent finding in all of Hall's studies of longtime dream diaries. The most dramatic results are found in a series of dreams that spans fifty-three years, from the age of twenty-five to a few days before the dreamer's death in 1965 at the age of seventy-eight. Hall did a detailed analysis of the first five decades of these dreams:

She dreamed about her parents and siblings with the same consistency throughout the fifty years, although her father died when she was very young and her mother died when Dorothea was 61. The number of aggressive and friendly interactions Dorothea had with various classes of characters did not change appreciably throughout the years.[30]

Nor did the basic themes of her dreams change. For five decades she was eating food in one out of every five dreams, losing something that belonged to her in one out of six dreams, being in a disorderly room or a room invaded by others in one out of ten dreams, and being late or missing a bus or train in one out of every sixteen dreams. And she was as likely to dream about the past when she was twenty-six as when she was seventy-six, suggesting that in dream life, at least, younger people are as likely to live in the past as older people.[31]

If there are impressive consistencies in long dream series, there are equally striking commonalities in the sets of dreams that have been gathered from societies around the world. Aside from the aforementioned sex differences in the ratio of male and female characters in men's and women's dreams, it has been found that there is usually more aggression than friendliness in everyone's dreams, that people are more often victims unless they are men over thirty, and that emotions like fear, anger, confusion, and anxiety predominate over positive emotions.[32] The news from the world of dreams is grim for most people everywhere, although there are exceptions to the rule.

For all the similarities in the dreams of men and women around the world, however, there also are notable individual differences when long dream series are compared to each other and to the typical findings for normative samples of men and women. If the hypothesis is made that unusually high or low frequencies in dream content categories are evidence for personal preoccupations, then these differences can be used to make inferences about personality characteristics. Hall's analysis of the thirty-seven dreams that Franz Kafka wrote in his diaries and letters over many years provides a good demonstration of this point.[33]

First, there is an unusually high number of body parts and disfigured bodies in Kafka's dreams. This finding is congruent with his excessive preoccupation with his body in waking life. He worried constantly about his physical health even before he became ill with tuberculosis, compared his body to the bodies of other men to his own disadvantage, and was interested in nudism and nature cures. His friend and first biographer, Max Brod, wrote that "every imperfection of the body tormented him."[34] Then, there is also a very frequent mention of clothing in Kafka's dreams, and Kafka was indeed extremely interested in clothes. His diaries are filled with descriptions of what people were wearing, and he always was very well dressed.

In addition, one of the most frequent activities in Kafka's dreams is merely "looking" or "watching," and he is lower than the typical male on aggressive and sexual interactions, personal success, and physical activities. This suggests a passive personality, and this is how he is described by Brod. Moreover, Kafka characterized himself as being timid, weak, hesitant, and lacking in confidence.[35] Kafka's personality as revealed in his dreams seems to have characteristics necessary for a writer in that he is a close observer, particularly of people, and he likes passive activities.[36]

Perhaps the most interesting example of how this method

reveals personality differences can be found in a comparison of the two greatest dream theorists of the twentieth century, Freud and Jung.[37] We have twenty-eight of Freud's dreams because he used his own dreams as examples in *The Interpretation of Dreams,* and thirty-one of Jung's dreams because they are an essential feature of his autobiographical study, *Memories, Dreams, Reflections,* which is also an invaluable case study of how important dreams can be in shaping a person's life.

First, there are more people in Freud's dreams even though Jung's dream reports are longer. Jung's dreams are filled with descriptions of scenery, architecture, and objects rather than people. This seemingly mundane finding, which could only emerge from looking at the dreams as a whole, fits with what is known about the two men. Freud was a highly sociable person; Jung was much more solitary and kept most would-be followers at a distance. He loved to pore over old manuscripts, and he was a lover of nature. "Today as then [meaning childhood], I am a solitary," he wrote in *Memories, Dreams, Reflections.*[38]

There are also differences in whom the two men dreamed about. Jung dreamed more about family members, Freud more about friends and acquaintances. And it does seem to be the case that Freud looked persistently for intimacy outside his family. He had many close friends and disciples with whom he interacted on a regular basis.

The differences in the patterns of friendly and aggressive interactions within their dreams are even more revealing. First, in the case of friendliness, Jung initiates every such interaction in his dreams—he is a befriender of others. Freud, on the other hand, initiates only three of the eleven friendly interactions in which he is involved—he is the befriended. This fits with what is known about the two men: Jung was much more active in social relations when he engaged in them, Freud more passive.

Second, there is a striking contrast in Freud's and Jung's

patterns of aggressive and friendly encounters with male and female characters. The typical male, as already noted, is aggressive with male characters and friendly with females. Jung fits that pattern when it comes to aggression; he is aggressive with about one in every four male characters he encounters in his dreams, and never at all with females. When it comes to friendliness, he differs only slightly from the norm in that he has an equal number of friendly interactions with both males and females.

It is Freud who shows the unusual interaction pattern on friendliness and aggression. In Freud's dreams, the typical pattern is reversed. He has an aggressive encounter with one in every four female characters, and almost none with males. On the other hand, he has many more friendly interactions with males than with females. In Freudian terms, Freud had an inverted Oedipus complex.

In keeping with these dream findings, there is reason to believe that Freud had hostile feelings toward women and unusually friendly feelings toward men. Many people—and not the least, feminists—have pointed to evidence in Freud's letters, comments to colleagues, and theories that he had a negative attitude toward women. His biographer, Ernest Jones, called his attitude toward women "old-fashioned." As to his relation to men, Freud wrote that "the affection of a group of courageous young men is the most precious gift that psychoanalysis has bestowed upon me." When a new man moved into the small inner circle around Freud, Freud gave him a ring. Jones wrote that in his self-analysis Freud had to overcome his "mental bi-sexuality."[39]

These findings not only reveal basic personality differences between the two men, but they may also shed light on the deeper reasons for the break that ended their several years of close intellectual collaboration. Freud, with his highly outgoing nature and desire for the friendship of men, wanted very much to anoint Jung as the person who would carry psychoanalysis into the next generation. Jung, with his more solitary nature, preference for family members, and more typical pattern of conflict with other males, resisted Freud's desire for greater closeness. Freud may have wanted an intellectual son to carry on his work, but Jung did not want another father.

For all the suggestiveness of these examples of how dream content relates to personality in long dream series, they are only examples. Quantitative content analysis has given us a fair idea of what people dream about, but more systematic work has to be done on how these content categories relate to the personality characteristics studied through tests and experimental studies before skeptics will sit up and take notice. The study of dream content and personality has barely begun.

Interest in the why, when, and what of dreams pales beside concern with the "meaning" of individual dreams. Starting with Freud, several rival theories and methods for interpreting dreams have been developed. They seem to differ so fundamentally, based as they are on very different assumptions about the basic determinants of human behavior, that bewildered outsiders who try to figure out what is going on often come to doubt whether dreams really have any meaning at all.

Freud, for example, claimed that dreams are disguised attempts at wish fulfillment, usually infantile wishes repressed from consciousness. He had his patients free-associate to individual elements of the dream to uncover these wishes and reconstruct the processes of the "dream work" that had transformed the unacceptable "latent thoughts" into the acceptable "manifest content" that allowed sleep to continue. The interpretation of dreams was an exercise in deciphering censored material, and the basic reality that Freud invariably found was in such bodily instincts as sex, hunger, and aggression.[40]

Jung, on the other hand, concluded that dreams are not an

attempt to conceal, but rather an effort to reveal deep insights about our personalities. He believed that dreams express the undeveloped parts of our psyches, speaking in an age-old symbolic language that has been sadly neglected by our overly rationalistic and secular modern civilization. He and his patients used myths and religious texts from all over the world to discover the symbolic wisdom that dreams contain as messages from a "collective unconscious" that is the storehouse of human experience. According to Jung, the meaning of dreams is usually a spiritual one, not a bodily one.[41]

Still another theory is possible. Medard Boss, an existential-phenomenological psychiatrist who studied with both Freud and Jung, believed that it was philosophical nonsense to speak of dreams as disguising wishes or expressing wisdom. Rejecting the concepts of the unconscious and symbolization as relics of a dead God, Boss wrote that dreams are simply another form of being-in-the-world. They present the way we view ourselves and the world if we will but look at them without the usual scientific preconceptions. This is accomplished by reflecting on three basic questions. What phenomena appear in the dream? How does the dreamer respond to these phenomena? How is the dreamer affected emotionally by these phenomena? By working through these three questions, we realize the obvious meaning of the dream because we are basically conscious and rational beings.[42]

To make the range of disagreement completely clear, it is only necessary to contrast the first three views with the gestalt or holistic approach developed by Fritz Perls, who criticized any attempt to understand the meaning of dreams intellectually, whether through free associations, symbol interpretations, or questions. He asserted that most dreams are manifestations of conflicts between various layers of the personality. They must be experienced emotionally to learn their meaning. Perls had members of his dream groups act out the various parts of the dream in an emotional way in the here and now in order to free the frozen energy sustaining the conflicts and thereby integrate the layers of the personality into a more harmonious whole.[43]

It would be possible to describe other theorists who provide variants or combinations of these four basic theories, but that would only compound the confusion, not end it. It does not help to know that the Marxist dream theorist and psychoanalyst Erich Fromm agreed with Freud on some things and with Jung on others, while arguing that the meaning of many dreams has to be sought in the alienating nature of what he thought to be the basic reality of our existence, the capitalist social system.[44] Nor does it make things any clearer to say that some latter-day Freudians, like Nandor Fodor and Angel Garma, became symbol interpreters who found basic dream meanings in such events as birth and intrauterine existence, while still other Freudians, like Thomas French and Erika Fromm, came to talk in terms of the "ego strengths" and present-day conflicts that are found in dreams, thereby sounding more like Boss or Erich Fromm (no relation to Erika) than Fodor or Garma.[45]

Still, appearances to the contrary, all this conflict has added to our understanding of the meaning of dreams. First, it has provided us with several methods for interpreting dreams. The methods that are associated with Freud, Jung, Boss, or Perls can be used by dream analysts of any theoretical persuasion. One does not have to be a Freudian, for example, to use the method of free association to discover the thoughts from the day before and the past that are connected with specific elements of a dream. Nor does one have to believe Perls's theories in order to have dreamers act out or dramatize their dreams to gain a better understanding of them. The methods are more theory-free than the warring schools of thought are willing to admit, and they all have the potential to provide useful information. How that information is interpreted is another story, of course, and that is where the basic assumptions of each theory come into play.

The ongoing conflict over the meaning of dreams also has advanced our understanding by inspiring the kind of systematic studies of dream content that were reported above. This work shows beyond the shadow of a doubt that there are patterns, consistencies, and thus "meanings" in dreams, thereby refuting the uninformed claims of physiological reductionists and computer enthusiasts who think that dream contents are the random firings of a machine set on recharge.[46] At the same time, this work does not allow us to go beyond the generalization that we dream about our concerns and preoccupations, or "uncompleted business," whether that uncompleted business be infantile wishes, undeveloped parts of our psyches, conflicts between parts of our personalities, present-day social conflicts, or plans about the future. It has not allowed us to pick and choose among the various dream theorists except on a few isolated issues.

What we can distill from the conflicting theories, then, is the notion that dreams are a type of thinking during sleep that presents our wishes, fears, feelings, thoughts, and ideas in the form of images and perceptions. These imagined experiences that we call dreams can be translated back into the conceptions of our waking language through such methods as free association, hypnosis, symbol interpretation, emotional reexperiencing, dream dramatization, and quantitative content analysis. From this perspective, Hall's characterization of dreams as a succession of images, usually visual, that express our conceptions of ourselves, our family, and our friends is all the general theory we need.[47] From there we can go on to determine whether the ideas of Freud, Jung, Boss, Perls, Fromm, or some other theorist illuminate the dream or dream series that interests us at the moment. In this view, the meaning of dreams is found in the fact that they are "the kaleidoscope of the mind":

Dreams objectify that which is subjective, they visualize that which is invisible, they transform the abstract into the concrete, and they make conscious that which is unconscious. They come from the most archaic alcoves of the mind as well as from the peripheral levels of waking consciousness. They are the kaleidoscope of the mind.[48]

We do know something about what people dream about, and we do have every reason to believe that dreams have meaning in terms of our preoccupations and personalities. For the most part, though, what is revealed by my overview of our knowledge of dreams is how little we really know. Dreams and dreaming remain largely a mystery to us. We don't know why or when we dream. We have only a rough idea of why some people remember a few dreams every once in a while and others remember several every morning. Even when we think we can discern the meaning in a dream, we do not know why we had that dream and not another, or why we used one particular image in the dream and not another. Sometimes we can free-associate until we are blue in the face, or check every element of the dream in mythical and religious texts, or imagine talking with the characters who were in the dream, and still have no idea as to why we had that particular dream.

Furthermore, for all our fascination with dreams, progress in solving their mysteries will be slow. As mere verbal reports on memories of imagined experiences that supposedly happened during the night and over which we have little or no control, dreams have a logical and experiential status like no other mental or behavioral event in the human sciences. At least, medical researchers are receiving immediate and ongoing verbal reports when a subject reports the private experience of a headache or a stomachache. At least, social psychologists can observe facial expressions or other nonverbal cues of private emotional states such as sadness or joy, which supplement the verbal reports that they receive. And certain dreamlike private experiences such as hallucinations sometimes can be induced in the laboratory with drugs.

But with dreams, none of these options is available. There can be no ongoing report of the experience; attempts to teach subjects to sleeptalk during dreams have failed.[49] There are few if any behavioral cues of what is being experienced when the dream is going on (even in the sleep laboratory, it is hard to hear laughing or to create the lighting needed to see smiles or grimaces). And you can't make dreams happen.

Since you can't see them and you can't make them happen, you have to wait for dreams to occur naturally. Then you have to hope that dreamers will be willing and able to talk about them. There is also the problem that dreamers may embellish their dreams, or leave parts out, or even make them up. Now, two different studies suggest that it is possible to tell a set of made-up dreams from real dreams, and it doesn't matter much for most studies if parts of the dream are not remembered or reported, but all this uncertainty is more than most social scientists can tolerate.[50] They like to be able to manipulate and observe their object of study.

Dreams can be collected in the laboratory setting, of course. But it is very tedious and wearing to be up for several hours each night, especially to awaken people who usually decide they don't like being awakened after all. It also can be very destructive of personal relationships to stay at a laboratory many nights a week. Most people are at home at night, and they prefer dream researchers to be with them there. In short, dreams are difficult to study in the laboratory because they happen when everybody should be at home sleeping.

If all that weren't enough in the way of unique problems, there is the further obstacle that dreams have been in effect ruled out of order as a fit object of scientific inquiry by the dominant paradigms within psychology. The behavioristic model derived from the philosophy of positivism insists that psychology must be defined as the study of behavior in order to rescue it from subjectivistic sentimentalizing and past associations with the mind, soul, and other concerns of old-fashioned philosophy and religion. True, dreams have standing as verbal reports within this scheme of things, but they are pretty much reduced to third-class citizenship when it is added that the verbal reports are of memories of imagined experiences that allegedly occurred during sleep. As for cognitive psychology, which does study thinking, it is so abstract and rationalistic that it has no use for the irrationality and emotionality of a thought process like dreaming. Such a state of affairs does not encourage new thinking and research on the topic. Dreams are outcasts in the groves of academe because they do not fit into the prevailing thought ways of respectable opinion. Even the new association with the laboratory has not been enough to overcome this pariah standing.

It is in the context of how little we know about dreams, and how slowly we are going to learn more, that we should consider the contribution Stewart's ideas have made to the study of dreams. In doing so, we could make much of Stewart's manifest failings as a data-gathering social scientist and a careful theorist. He did misunderstand Senoi dream theory and Senoi dream practices, and he did let his imagination run away from him when he made claims in the fifties that were patently contradicted by the dreams that he recorded in the appendix of his own dissertation. In this sense he was more a romantic storyteller than the social scientist and theorist he wanted to be.

But in an area where little is known and the dominant scientific paradigms discourage sustained research, it may be better to have new and testable ideas than no ideas at all, even if the source of those ideas turns out to be very different from what the originator claims. As the history of the laboratory work on dreams reminds us, it can be as useful to stimulate new research directions as it is to be right.[51]

Whatever their source, Kilton Stewart did put forth ideas that have triggered further investigations of dreams in both psychology and anthropology. They may or may not prove to be very important in the long run, but we should remember that they have been useful for a few people even if the jury is still out on the degree to which they can be put to work by people in general.

Just as nature abhors a vacuum, so too does the human psyche. As long as dreams remain a mystery, new mystiques and allegories about them will continue to develop, and, of necessity, they will reflect the problems of our times and our basic assumptions about human nature. Until there is a more systematic body of theory and research on dreams, there may be almost as many dream theories as there are dreamers. These dream theories will serve as our mirrors, just as anthropological accounts of tribal peoples often do. They will reveal our conceptions of our society as surely as the dreams themselves reveal our conceptions of ourselves, our families, and our friends.

But each new mystique may also give us further insights about dreams. We gradually may accumulate better theories about dreams through our mystiques if we keep reminding ourselves that they are allegorical stories as well as general theories and if we cultivate our historical awareness as well as search for timeless concepts and principles. The imagination of a Kilton Stewart can be combined with the rigor of disciplined scientific thinkers to provide testable hypotheses for the next generation of dream detectives.

However, along with being skeptical, we must remember to enjoy our scientific allegories. They are pleasurable while we are believing them, and they are fun to analyze and scandalous to read about when we begin to see through them. They tell us about ourselves in a whimsical way.

The saga of that quintessential American dreamer, Kilton R. Stewart, is as familiar to us as Paul Bunyan, apple pie, B. F. Skinner, or the search for utopia in an idyllic country setting. Even so, it has added to our store of ideas about dreams by suggesting that they can be a basis for group harmony and individual creativity as well as a royal road to the unconscious.

Notes

1 The New Mystique of Dreams

1. M. Ullman, S. Krippner, and A. Vaughan, *Dream Telepathy* (Baltimore: Penguin Books, 1973), p. 24.

2. E.g., C. S. Hall, "Diagnosing Personality by the Analysis of Dreams," *Journal of Abnormal and Social Psychology* 42 (1947):68–79; C. S. Hall, "What People Dream About," *Scientific American* 184 (1951):60–63; C. S. Hall, *The Meaning of Dreams* (New York: Harper & Row, 1953); C. S. Hall and R. L. Van de Castle, *The Content Analysis of Dreams* (New York: Appleton-Century-Crofts, 1966); C. S. Hall and V. J. Nordby, *The Individual and His dreams* (New York: New American Library, 1972).

3. S. Freud, *Introductory Lectures on Psychoanalysis* (1915–16), *The Standard Edition of the Complete Psychological Works of Sigmund Freud,* 24 vols., trans. James Strachey (London: Hogarth Press, 1963), 15:86–87.

4. F. Crick and G. Mitchison, "The Function of Dream Sleep," *Nature* 304 (1983):111–14; C. Evans, *Landscape of the Night: How and Why We Dream* (New York: Viking Press, 1984).

5. D. Bryant, *The Kin of Ata Are Waiting for You* (Berkeley: Moon Books, 1971); U. K. Leguin, *The Word for World Is Forest* (New York: Berkley Publishing, 1972).

6. N. Kleitman, *Sleep and Wakefulness* (Chicago: University of Chicago Press, 1963), ch. 11; W. Dement, *Some Must Watch While Some Must Sleep* (San Francisco: W. H. Freeman & Co., 1974).

7. Jungian-Senoi Institute, Berkeley, Calif., Introductory Pamphlet, 1982, p. 1.

8. K. R. Stewart, "Dream Theory in Malaya," *Complex,* no. 6 (1951):21–33; K. R. Stewart, "Culture and Personality in Two Primitive Groups," *Complex,* no. 9 1953–54):3–23; K. R. Stewart, "Mental Hygiene and World Peace," *Mental Hygiene* 38 (1954):387–407; K. R. Stewart, "The Dream Comes of Age," *Mental Hygiene* 46 (1962):230–37.

9. S. Krippner and W. Hughes, "Genius at Work," *Psychology Today,* June 1970, pp. 40–43; K. Goodall, "Dream and Tell for the Fuller Life," *Psychology Today,* June 1972, p. 32; R. D. Cartwright, "Happy Endings for Our Dreams," *Psychology Today,* December 1978, pp. 66–67.

10. Stewart, "Dream Theory in Malaya," pp. 33, 28.

11. P. Garfield, *Creative Dreaming* (New York: Ballantine Books, 1974) p. 83.

12. Ibid., p. 84.

13. Stewart, "Mental Hygiene and World Peace," p. 396.

14. Garfield, *Creative Dreaming,* p. 81.

15. Stewart, "Dream Theory in Malaya," p. 27.

16. Ibid., pp. 26–27; Garfield, *Creative Dreaming,* pp. 84–87.

17. Stewart, "Dream Theory in Malaya," pp. 22, 21–22.

2 The Senoi and Their Dream Theory

1. R. K. Dentan, *The Semai: A Nonviolent People of Malaya* (New York: Holt, Rinehart & Winston, 1968), ch. 1; R. K. Dentan, "Senoi Dream Praxis," *Dream Network Bulletin* 2 (5) (May 1983):1–3; G. Benjamin, "Themes in Malayan Cultural Ecology," paper presented at the Conference on Cultural Values and Tropical Ecology, East-West Environment and Policy Centers, Honolulu, June 2–10, 1983; K. Endicott, *Bateg Negrito Religion* (New York: Oxford University Press, 1979).

2. "Malaysia, Federation of," *New Columbia Encyclopedia* (New York: Columbia University Press, 1975), pp. 1670–71.

3. Dentan, *The Semai,* p. 1.

4. H. D. Noone, "Report on the Settlements and Welfare of the Ple-Temiar Senoi of the Perak-Kelantan Watershed," *Journal of the Federated Malay States Museums* 19, pt. 1 (December 1936):26.

5. Dentan, *The Semai,* p. 31.

6. P. D. R. Williams-Hunt, *An Introduction to the Malayan Aborigine* (Kuala Lumpur: Government Press, 1952), pp. 49–50; Dentan, *The Semai,* pp. 31–33, 44–45, 50–53.

7. Dentan, *The Semai,* pp. 21, 69, 80–81, 93–95, 103; C. Robarchek, "Learning to Fear: A Case Study of Emotional Conditioning," *American Ethnologist* 6 (1979):556.

8. R. K. Dentan, "A Dream of Senoi," Special Studies Series, Council on International Studies, State University of New York at Buffalo (1984), p. 9.

9. R. Noone, with D. Holman, *In Search of the Dream People* (New York: William Morrow, 1972).

10. R. K. Dentan, "Notes on Childhood in a Nonviolent Context: The Semai Case," in *Learning Non-Aggression,* ed. A. Montague (New York: Oxford University Press, 1978), p. 95.

11. R. Noone, *In Search of the Dream People,* pp. 169ff.

12. Ibid., p. 23.

13. Dentan, "Notes on Childhood," p. 98.

14. R. Noone, *In Search of the Dream People,* p. 39.

15. A. G. Fix, *The Demography of the Semai Senoi* (Ann Arbor: Museum of Anthropology, No. 62, 1977), pp. 60–62; Dentan, "Notes on Childhood," p. 111.

16. Dentan, "Dream of Senoi," p. 9.

17. J. D. Kinzie and J. M. Bolton, "Psychiatry with the Aborigines of West Malaysia," *American Journal of Psychiatry* 130 (1973): 767–73.

18. Dentan, "Notes on Childhood," p. 128.

19. Robarchek, "Learning to Fear," p. 560.

20. Dentan, *The Semai,* p. 22; Robarchek, "Learning to Fear," p. 558.

21. Dentan, *The Semai,* p. 23; Robarchek, "Learning to Fear," p. 5.

22. Robarchek, "Learning to Fear," pp. 558, 563.

23. Dentan, *The Semai,* p. 60; Robarchek, "Learning to Fear," pp. 560–62.

24. Robarchek, "Learning to Fear," p. 556.

25. Dentan, *The Semai,* p. 55.

26. Dentan, "Dream of Senoi," pp. 21–23; Dentan, "Senoi Dream Praxis," pp. 2–3.

27. Geoffrey Benjamin, pers. com., June 16, 1983.

28. Ibid.

29. Dentan, "Dream of Senoi," pp. 26, 39; Dentan, "Senoi Dream Praxis," pp. 2–3.

30. J. S. Lincoln, *The Dream in Primitive Cultures* (Baltimore: Williams & Wilkins, 1935). For a recent account of a tribal dream theory

with many parallels to that of the Senoi, see T. Gregor, "Far Far Away My Shadow Wandered . . . : The Dream Theories of the Mehinaku Indians of Brazil," *American Ethnologist* 8 (1981):709–20.

31. Dentan, *The Semai,* p. 19; for other evidence on the role of dreams in Senoi culture, see ibid., pp. 41, 61, 68, 83–85, 88, and 94. Dentan also mentions the role of dreams in "Notes on Childhood," pp. 100–101, 121.

32. C. G. Jung, "On the Nature of Dreams," in C. G. Jung, *Dreams* (Princeton: Princeton University Press, 1974), pp. 290–91; E. R. Dodds, *The Greeks and the Irrational* (Berkeley: University of California Press, 1951), p. 107; D. M. Guss, "Steering for Dream: Dream Concepts of the Makiritare Indians of Venezuela," *Journal of Latin American Folklore* 6 (1980):28.

33. Dentan, "Senoi Dream Praxis," p. 2.

34. Dentan, "Dream of Senoi," p. 33.

35. Ibid., pp. 34–35, 28–29.

36. Clayton Robarchek, personal communication, June 10, 1983.

37. Dentan, "Dream of Senoi," p. 33.

38. Robarchek, "Learning to Fear," p. 561.

39. Ibid.

40. Dentan, "Senoi Dream Praxis," p. 2.

41. Dentan, *The Semai,* p. 85.

42. Williams-Hunt, *Introduction to the Malayan Aborigine,* pp. 49–50.

43. Dentan, "Senoi Dream Praxis," p. 3; Benjamin, personal communication, June 16, 1983; Robarchek, personal communication, June 10, 1983.

44. Dentan, "Senoi Dream Praxis," p. 12.

45. C. Robarchek, "Conflict, Emotion, and Abreaction," *Ethos* 7 (1979):198.

46. Ibid., p. 112.

47. Benjamin, personal communication, June 16, 1983.

48. Dentan, *The Semai,* p. 3; Dentan, "Notes on Childhood," p. 129.

49. I. Carey, *Tenleg of Kui Serok* (Kuala Lumpur: Dewan Bahasa, 1961), p. 2.

50. G. Benjamin, "Temiar Social Groupings," *Federation Museums Journal* 11, n.s. (1966):7.

51. G. Benjamin, "Temiar-Kinship," *Federation Museums Journal* 12, n.s. (1967):20.

52. Dentan, letter to the author, May 19, 1983; Benjamin, personal communication, June 16, 1983.

53. Noone, *In Search of the Dream People,* p. 28.

54. A. Faraday and J. Wren-Lewis, "The Selling of the Senoi," *Dream Network Bulletin* 3–4 (March–April 1984):2.

55. E. B. Tylor, *Primitive Culture,* 2 vols. (New York: Harper & Row, 1958), 2:22ff.; this book was first published in 1871.

56. G. Roheim, *The Gates of the Dream* (New York: International Universities Press, 1952).

57. For information on the role of dreams in healing practices in tribal societies, see Lincoln, *Dream in Primitive Cultures;* G. Roheim, *The Eternal Ones of the Dream* (New York: International Universities Press, 1945); R. G. D'Andrade, "Anthropological Studies of Dreams," in *Psychological Anthropology,* ed. F. L. K. Hsu (Homewood, Ill.: Dorsey Press, 1961); C. W. O'Nell, *Dreams, Culture, and the Individual* (San Francisco: Chandler & Sharp, 1976); W. Kracke, "Dreaming in Kagwahiv: Dream Beliefs and Their Psychic Uses in an Amazonian Culture," *Psychoanalytic Study of Society* 8 (1979):119–71; B. Tedlock, "Quiche Maya Dream Interpretation," *Ethos* 9 (1981):313–30; L. G. Peters, "Trance, Induction, and Psychotherapy in Nepalese Tamang Shamanism," *American Ethnologist* 9 (1982): 21–46.

3 The Magic of Kilton Stewart

1. C. Parsons, *Vagabondage* (London: Chatto & Windus, 1941), p. 151.

2. Ibid., pp. 152–53.

3. Ibid., pp. 157–58.

4. Ibid., p. 178.

5. Ibid., p. 233.

6. Interview with Omer C. Stewart, Boulder, Colorado, July 1, 1983.

7. Interview with Dorothy Nyswander and Margaret Nyswander Manson, Kensington, Calif., July 27, 1983.

8. S. D. Porteus, *Primitive Intelligence and Environment* (New York: Macmillan, 1937), ch. 27.

9. K. R. Stewart, "Journey of a Psychologist," unpublished manuscript (1936), p. 337; this manuscript was kindly provided by Omer C. Stewart.

10. Ibid., p. 338.

11. Letter to the author from Omer C. Stewart, June 12, 1983.

12. Interview with Dorothy Nyswander, Kensington, Calif., July 27, 1983.

13. Telephone interview with John Wires, Plainfield, Vt., December 18, 1983.

14. E. Perry, "Dr. Kilton Stewart Says Dreams Have Meaning," *Cliff Dweller* 1 (August 1964):4.

15. Interview with Omer C. Stewart, Boulder, Colorado, July 1, 1983; Omer is six years younger than Kilton.

16. Letter from Sir Edmund R. Leach, June 11, 1983.

17. Stewart, "Journey of a Psychologist," p. 467.

18. Ibid., p. 471.

19. H. D. Noone, "Report on the Settlements and Welfare of the Ple-Temiar Senoi of the Perah-Kelantan Watershed," *Journal of the Federated Malay States Museums* 19, pt. 1 (1936):13; see p. 8 for information on the expeditions.

20. Stewart, "Journey of a Psychologist," p. 507.

21. Ibid., p. 506.

22. E. Menaker, *Otto Rank: A Rediscovered Legacy* (New York: Columbia University Press, 1982); O. Rank, *Will Therapy* (New York: Alfred A. Knopf, 1936).

23. J. Taft, *Otto Rank* (New York: Julian Press, 1958), pp. 180–97, 205; P. Bailey, "The Psychological Center, Paris, 1934," *Journal of the Otto Rank Association* 2 (1967):10–25.

24. E. James Lieberman, author of a good and detailed account of Rank's life, *Acts of Will: The Life and Work of Otto Rank* (New York: Free Press, 1985), told me in a telephone interview on July 25, 1984, that Bailey was the only person close to Rank who might have been practicing in Paris in the summer of 1935. Information in *Who's Who In America* in the fifties and in "Pearce Bailey, Neurologist," *New York Times,* June 28, 1976, shows that Bailey remained in Paris until 1936.

25. This account of Stewart's travel schedule in 1935 is based upon correspondence from the time that was provided by Omer C. Stewart.

26. Parsons, *Vagabondage,* p. 179.

27. Ibid.

28. Ibid.

29. The information on plans to pursue a Ph.D. and the change in schools was found in correspondence from the time provided by Omer C. Stewart.

30. In a letter dated June 28, 1983, Sir Edmund R. Leach very kindly provided me with this information about the change in Noone's dissertation title. He obtained it from the official records of Cambridge University.

31. H. D. Noone, "Chinchem: A Study of the Role of Dream Experience in Culture-Contact Amongst the Temiar Senoi of Malaya," *Man,* April 1939, p. 57; my thanks to Sir Edmund R. Leach for providing this reference.

32. W. LaBarre, *The Ghost Dance* (New York: Doubleday, 1970), p. 13.

33. K. R. Stewart, "A Psychological Analysis of the Negritos of Luzon, Philippine Islands," *Man,* January 1939, p. 10; my thanks to Sir Edmund R. Leach for providing this reference.

34. For many similar romantic illusions by other American visitors to the USSR and other communist countries, see Paul Hollander, *Political Pilgrims: Travels of Western Intellectuals in the Soviet Union, China, and Cuba, 1928–1978* (New York: Oxford University Press, 1981).

35. K. R. Stewart, "The Yami of Botel Tobago," *Philippine Magazine,* July 1937, p. 304.

36. Ibid., p. 323.

37. R. Noone, with D. Holman, *In Search of the Dream People* (New York: William Morrow, 1972); quotes from letters Pat Noone wrote to his parents that suggest his early interest in Senoi mental health and their ideas about dreams; see pp. 22–36.

38. A letter to the author from Claudia Parsons, July 30, 1983, provided this information on how Stewart's data were preserved and retrieved.

39. This information comes from two sources, a written chronology of Kilton Stewart's life provided by Omer C. Stewart and an interview with Omer C. Stewart, July 1, 1983.

40. Interview with Clara Flagg, November 26, 1983.

41. K. R. Stewart, "Magico-Religious Beliefs and Practices in

Primitive Society—A Sociological Interpretation of Their Therapeutic Aspects," unpublished Ph.D. dissertation, London School of
Economics, 1946, p. 71.

42. Ibid., p. 244.

43. Ibid., p. 118.

44. Information on how Stewart collected dreams among the
Yami comes from letters to the author from Sir Edmund R. Leach,
June 11, 1983, and from Nancy Grasby, August 8, 1983.

45. Stewart, "Magico-Religious Beliefs," pp. 92, 118, 140.

46. Evidence on how Stewart collected dreams among natives in
the Philippines comes from two sources. First, on pp. 255–56 of the
dissertation Stewart writes that he lived for a month at the Bataan
Farm School and another month at the Zambales Negrito Farm
School. Second, there are numerous mentions of schools and
English-speaking natives in his *Pygmies and Dream Giants* (New
York: W. W. Norton, 1954). This book is a novellike account of his
adventures in the Philippines. Omer Stewart believes it is an amalgamation of his several visits to the Philippines and that it is based
in part on his 1936 autobiography, "Journey of a Psychologist." The
evidence on how Stewart collected dreams while in the Philippines
can be found on pp. 29–31, 101, 121, 129, 173, 206–11, and 255.

47. G. W. Domhoff, "Night Dreams and Hypnotic Dreams: Is
There Evidence That They Are Different?" *International Journal of
Clinical and Experimental Hypnosis* 12 (1964):159–68; C. Tart, "A
Comparison of Suggested Dreams Occurring in Hypnosis and
Sleep," *International Journal of Clinical and Experimental Hypnosis* 12
(1964):263–80; D. Barrett, "The Hypnotic Dream: Its Relation to
Nocturnal Dreams and Waking Fantasies," *Journal of Abnormal Psy-
chology* 88 (1979):584–91. For a reprinting of the classic studies on
hypnotic dreams and a good commentary on the issue by the edi-
tor, see C. S. Moss, ed., *The Hypnotic Investigation of Dreams* (New
York: John Wiley, 1967).

48. The information concerning Stewart's membership in the
Royal Anthropological Institute came to me in a letter from the
secretary to the director, Windsor Sylvester, dated September
2, 1983.

49. The fact that Stewart was not a research fellow of the Rockefeller Institute was communicated to me in a letter from J. William

Hess, associate director of the Rockefeller Archive Center, July 18, 1983. The actual nature of Stewart's employment in Peking was explained to me by Professor Francis L. K. Hsu, who was a social worker there at the time, in a telephone interview on August 29, 1983. However, S. D. Porteus did use a grant he obtained from the Rockefeller Foundation to pay for part of Stewart's travels for a year or two, which may have been the basis for Stewart's larger claim.

50. Stewart, "Magico-Religious Beliefs," pp. 1, 52–53, 83, 92; K. R. Stewart, "Dream Theory in Malaya," *Complex,* no. 6 (1951):23.

51. Stewart, "Dream Theory in Malaya," p. 25.

52. Ibid., pp. 25–26.

53. Ibid., pp. 25, 26.

54. Stewart, "Magico-Religious Beliefs," p. 476 (dream no. 193).

55. Ibid., p. 475 (dream no. 190).

56. Ibid., p. 460 (dream no. 95); p. 462 (dream no. 109); p. 467 (dream no. 143), and p. 477 (dream no. 195).

57. Stewart, "Dream Theory in Malaya," p. 27.

58. Stewart, "Magico-Religious Beliefs," pp. 151–52.

59. Stewart, "Yami of Botel Tobago"; K. R. Stewart, "Education and Split Personalities," *Mental Hygiene* 27 (1943):430–38; K. R. Stewart, "Mental Hygiene and World Peace," *Mental Hygiene* 38 (1954):387; and K. R. Stewart, "The Dream Comes of Age," *Mental Hygiene* 46 (1962):230–37.

4 The Appeal of Senoi Dream Theory

1. This information on how Senoi dream theory came to Esalen comes from telephone interviews with Tom Allen, Joe Kamiya, George Leonard, Edward Maupin, Michael Murphy, and Charles Tart in the fall of 1983.

2. W. T. Anderson, *The Upstart Spring: Esalen and the American Awakening* (Menlo Park, Calif.: Addison-Wesley, 1983), p. 122.

3. Ibid., chs. 8, 9, 10.

4. B. F. Skinner, *Walden Two* (New York: Macmillan, 1948). Much of the information in this paragraph comes from a telephone conversation with George Leonard on November 28, 1983. The se-

rialized material appeared in an article entitled "Visiting Day in the Year 2001 A.D.," *Look,* October 1, 1968, p. 47. Leonard received about 5,000 letters in response to the *Look* serialization and the book.

5. G. B. Leonard, *Education and Ecstasy* (New York: Delacorte Press, 1968), p. 194. Maslow may have revised his opinion considerably. When he came to Esalen in 1966 to give a series of seminars on his concept of "being language," he was taunted unmercifully by Fritz Perls. Perls began by challenging Maslow's claim that his massage in the Esalen hot spring baths by female masseuses was a "peak experience." "Bullshit," said Perls, "you are just turned on." When Maslow began his formal discussion using a question-and-answer approach, Perls interrupted by saying: "This is just like school. Here is the teacher, and there is the pupil, giving the right answer." Later, at the evening session, Perls began to crawl around on the floor, and Maslow told him he was being childish. So Perls made whining sounds and hugged Maslow's knees, as though Perls were at one of his own gestalt therapy sessions. Walter Anderson, who tells the story in his history of Esalen, then writes: "There sat kindly Maslow, a professor at Brandeis, the father of humanistic psychology, rigid as a rock in his crew cut and cashmere sweater while this crazy old man in a jump suit hugged his knees and made baby noises. 'This begins to look like sickness,' Maslow said." For the full account of this incredible encounter between Perls and Maslow, see Anderson, *Upstart Spring,* pp. 133–37.

6. Leonard, *Education and Ecstasy,* pp. 210, 196.

7. C. Tart, ed., *Altered States of Consciousness* (New York: John Wiley, 1969), p. 115.

8. K. Goodall, "Dream and Tell for a Fuller Life," *Psychology Today,* June 1972, p. 32; J. Latner and M. Sabini, "Working the Dream Factory: Social Dreamwork," *Voices* 18 (1972):38–43.

9. For a compilation of all the detailed evidence from journalists and anthropologists that Don Juan does not exist and that Carlos Castenada fabricated his account, see R. DeMille, ed., *The Don Juan Papers* (Santa Barbara: Ross-Erikson Publishers, 1980).

10. T. Roszak, *Where the Wasteland Ends* (Garden City, N.Y.: Doubleday, 1972), ch. 1.

11. Ibid., p. 83.

12. A. Faraday, *Dream Power* (New York: Coward, McCann, & Geoghegan, 1972), pp. 297–98; A. Faraday, *The Dream Game* (New York: Harper & Row, 1974), pp. 258–66.

13. P. Garfield, *Creative Dreaming* (New York: Ballantine Books, 1974), p. ix.

14. Ibid., p. 84.

15. "An Illusion Destroyed," *Human Nature,* June 1978, p. 12.

16. D. Meyer, *The Positive Thinkers* (Garden City, N.Y.: Doubleday, 1975); P. Rieff, *The Triumph of the Therapeutic* (New York: Harper & Row, 1966); B. Zilbergeld, *The Shrinking of America: Myths of Psychological Change* (Boston: Little, Brown, 1983).

17. J. T. Clifford, "On Ethnographic Allegory," in *The Making of Ethnographic Texts,* ed. J. T. Clifford and G. Marcus, School of American Research Publications, Santa Fe, N.M., forthcoming. See also J. T. Clifford, "On Ethnographic Authority," *Representations* 1 (1983):118–47.

18. E. Evans-Pritchard, *The Nuer* (Oxford: Clarendon Press, 1960), quoted in Clifford, "On Ethnographic Allegory," pp. 27–28.

19. M. Mead, *Coming of Age in Samoa* (New York: William Morrow, 1928), quoted in Clifford, "On Ethnographic Allegory," p. 9.

20. Clifford, "On Ethnographic Allegory," p. 9.

21. Ibid., p. 32.

5 The Efficacy of Senoi Dream Theory

1. C. S. Hall, "Ethnic Similarities in Manifest Dream Contents: A Modest Confirmation of the Theory of University Man," Institute of Dream Research (1967); T. Gregor, "A Content Analysis of Mehinaku Dreams," *Ethos* 9 (1981):353–90.

2. E. G. Werlin, "An Experiment in Elementary Education," in *Contemporary Educational Psychology,* ed. R. M. Jones (New York: Harper & Row, 1966), p. 233.

3. Jones, in ibid., pp. 248–49.

4. Ibid., p. 237.

5. Ibid., p. 238.

6. E. Greenleaf, "'Senoi' Dream Groups," *Psychotherapy: Theory, Research, and Practice* 10 (1973):218.

7. E.g., J. R. Gibb, "Effects of Human Relations Training," in *Handbook of Psychotherapy and Behavior Change,* ed. A. E. Bergin and S. L. Garfield (New York: John Wiley, 1971); J. Bebout and B. Grodon, "The Value of Encounter," in *Perspectives on Encounter Groups,* ed. L. Solomon and B. Berzon (San Francisco: Jossey-Bass, 1972); M. A. Lieberman, I. D. Yalom, and M. Miles, *Encounter Groups: First Facts* (New York: Basic Books, 1973); P. B. Smith, "Controlled Studies of the Outcomes of Sensitivity Training," *Psychological Bulletin* 82 (1974):597–622; A. Zander, "The Psychology of Group Processes," *Annual Review of Psychology* 30 (1979):417–51.

Most of these studies also show the importance of the leader in determining how members view the experience. A study by Dane Archer, "Power in Groups: Self-Concept Changes of Powerful and Powerless Group Members," *Journal of Applied Behavioral Sciences* 10 (1975):208–20, shows that the mixed results within some groups can be explained by power differentials within the group itself. Those who are perceived as powerful members of the group, as measured by a questionnaire about group interaction patterns, are the ones most likely to improve in self-concept from the group experience.

8. B. Zilbergeld, *The Shrinking of America: Myths of Psychological Change* (Boston: Little, Brown, 1983), pp. 114–21.

9. Greenleaf, "'Senoi' Dream Groups," p. 221.

10. Jones, in Werlin, "Experiment in Elementary Education," p. 237.

11. C. Tart, "From Spontaneous Event to Lucidity: A Review of Attempts to Consciously Control Nocturnal Dreaming," in *Handbook of Dreams,* ed. B. B. Wolman (New York: Van Nostrand Reinhold, 1979), p. 239.

12. These findings and many others from a variety of studies are summarized in A. M. Arkin and J. S. Antrobus, "The Effects of External Stimuli Applied Prior to and During Sleep on Sleep Experience," in *The Mind in Sleep,* ed. (A. M. Arkin, J. S. Antrobus, and S. J. Ellman (Hillsdale, N.J.: Lawrence Erlbaum Associates, 1978); the phrase "richly represented" appears on p. 65.

13. J. Stoyva, "Posthypnotically Suggested Dreams and the Sleep Cycle," *Archives of General Psychiatry* 12 (1965):287–94; C. Tart, "The Control of Nocturnal Dreaming by Means of Posthyp-

notic Suggestions," *International Journal of Parapsychology* 9 (1967):184–89; C. Tart and L. Dick, "Conscious Control of Dreaming: I. The Posthypnotic Dream," *Journal of Abnormal Psychology* 76 (1970):304–15.

14. T. X. Barker, P. C. Walker, and H. W. Hahn, Jr., "Effects of Hypnotic Induction and Suggestions on Nocturnal Dreaming and Thinking," *Journal of Abnormal Psychology* 82 (1973):414–27.

15. C. C. Hiew, "The Influence of Pre-Sleep Suggestions on Dream Content," paper presented to the New Brunswick Psychological Association Convention, October 24–25, 1974.

16. C. C. Hiew, "Individual Differences in the Control of Dreaming," paper presented to the Association for the Psychophysiological Study of Sleep, 1976.

17. C. C. Hiew and P. Short, "Emotional Involvement and Auditory Retrieval Cues in Pre-Sleep Dream Suggestion," paper presented to the Association for the Psychophysiological Study of Sleep, 1977.

18. R. Brunette and I. DeKonick. "The Effect of Pre-Sleep Suggestions Related to a Phobic Object on Dream Affect," abstract, Association for the Psychophysiological Study of Sleep, 1977.

19. P. Garfield, *Creative Dreaming* (New York: Ballantine Books, 1974), pp. 100–101; A. Faraday, *Dream Power* (New York: Coward, McCann, & Geoghegan, 1972), pp. 297–98; A. Faraday, *The Dream Game* (New York: Harper & Row, 1974), p. 260.

20. Tart, "From Spontaneous Event to Lucidity," p. 262.

21. B. L. Wollmering, "Dream Control for Behavioral Change," unpublished Ph.D. dissertation, University of Arizona, 1978.

22. R. D. Cartwright, "The Influence of a Conscious Wish on Dreams: A Methodological Study of Dream Meaning and Function," *Journal of Abnormal Psychology* 82 (1974):387–93.

23. R. D. Cartwright, "Happy Endings for Our Dreams," *Psychology Today*, December 1978, p. 66.

24. Tart, "From Spontaneous Event to Lucidity," pp. 259, 256–57.

25. Ibid., p. 259.

26. S. LaBerge, L. Nagel, W. Dement, and V. Zarcone, "Lucid Dreaming Verified by Volitional Communication During REM Sleep," *Perceptual and Motor Skills* 52 (1981):727–32.

27. K. Hearne, "Effects of Performing Certain Set Tasks in the Lucid-Dream State," *Perceptual and Motor Skills* 54 (1982):259–62.

28. K. Hearne, "Lucid Dream Induction," *Journal of Mental Imagery* 7 (1983):19–24; P. Tholey, "Techniques for Inducing and Manipulating Lucid Dreams," *Perceptual and Motor Skills* 57 (1983): 79–90.

29. J. Latner and M. Sabini, "Working the Dream Factory: Social Dreamwork," *Voices* 18 (1972):43.

30. P. Garfield, "Self-Conditioning of Dream Content," paper presented to the Association for the Psychophysiological Study of Sleep, 1974, as reported in Tart, "From Spontaneous Event to Lucidity," p. 241.

31. D. Foulkes and M. L. Griffin, "An Experimental Study of 'Creative Dreaming,'" *Sleep Research* 5 (1976):129.

32. M. L. Griffin and D. Foulkes, "Deliberate Presleep Control of Dream Content: An Experimental Study," *Perceptual and Motor Skills* 45 (1977):660–62.

33. R. Ogilvie, K. Belicki, and A. Nagy, "Voluntary Control of Dream Affect?" *Waking and Sleeping* 2 (1978):189–94.

34. K. R. Stewart, "The Dream Comes of Age," *Mental Hygiene* 46 (1962):235.

35. C. S. Hall and R. L. Van de Castle, *The Content Analysis of Dreams* (New York: Appleton-Century-Crofts, 1966).

36. Tart, "From Spontaneous Event to Lucidity," p. 262.

37. E.g., Michael J. Harner, *The Jivaro* (Garden City, N.Y.: Doubleday, 1972), pp. 136–38; W. Kracke, "Dreaming in Kagwahiv: Dream Beliefs and Their Psychic Uses in an Amazonian Culture," *Psychoanalytic Study of Society* 8 (1979):163–64. I am grateful to Professor Kracke for providing these anthropological examples of attempts at dream or vision control.

6 The Mystery of Dreams

1. S. Freud, *The Interpretation of Dreams* (1900), vols. 4–5, *The Standard Edition of the Complete Psychological Works of Sigmund Freud* (London: Hogarth Press, 1953), pp. 233–34, 578.

2. R. D. Cartwright, *Night Life* (Englewood Cliffs, N.J.: Prentice-Hall, 1977), chs. 4–7; F. Crick and G. Mitchison, "The

Function of Dream Sleep," *Nature* 304 (1983):111–14; C. Evans, *Landscape of the Night: How and Why We Dream* (New York: Viking Press, 1984).

3. W. R. Ashby, *Design for a Brain* (New York: John Wiley, 1960), p. 14.

4. E.g., R. Schonbar, "Some Manifest Personality Characteristics of Recallers and Non-Recallers," *Journal of Consulting Psychology* 23 (1959):414–18; C. Tart, "Frequency of Dream Recall and Some Personality Measures," *Journal of Consulting Psychology* 26 (1962):467–70; G. W. Domhoff and A. Gerson, "Replication and Critique of Three Studies on Personality Correlates of Dream Recall," *Journal of Consulting Psychology* 31 (1967):431; A. B. Hill, "Personality Correlates of Dream Recall," *Journal of Consulting Psychology* 42 (1974):766–73.

5. M. Hiscock and D. B. Cohen, "Visual Imagery and Dream Recall," *Journal of Research in Personality* 7 (1973):179–88; T. L. Cory, D. W. Ormiston, E. Simmel, and M. Dainoff, "Predicting the Frequency of Dream Recall," *Journal of Abnormal Psychology* 84 (1975):261–66; D. B. Cohen, "Toward a Theory of Dream Recall," *Psychological Bulletin* 81 (1974):138–54.

6. C. S. Hall and R. Raskin, "Do We Dream During Sleep?" privately printed monograph distributed to members of the Association for the Psychophysiological Study of Sleep, March 1980.

7. E.g., J. Kamiya, "Behavioral, Subjective, and Physiological Effects of Drowsiness and Sleep," in *Functions of Varied Experience,* ed. D. Fiske and S. Maddi (Homewood, Ill: Dorsey Press, 1961); D. Foulkes, "Dream Reports from Different Stages of Sleep," *Journal of Abnormal and Social Psychology* 65 (1962):14–25. For a summary of several studies, see C. S. Hall, "Caveat Lector!" *Psychoanalytic Review* 54 (1967):655–61.

8. E. Aserinsky and N. Kleitman, "Regularly Occurring Periods of Eye Motility and Concomitant Phenomena During Sleep," *Science* 118 (1953):273–74.

9. W. Dement, "Dream Recall and Eye Movements During Sleep in Schizophrenics and Normals," *Journal of Nervous and Mental Disease* 122 (1955):262–69; W. Dement and N. Kleitman, "Relation of Eye Movements During Sleep to Dream Activity: Objective Method for Study of Dreaming," *Journal of Experimental Psychology*

53 (1957):339–46; W. Dement and N. Kleitman, "Cyclic Variations in EEG During Sleep and Their Relation to Eye Movements, Body Motility, and Dreaming," *Electroencephalography and Clinical Neurophysiology* 9 (1957):673–90.

10. I was among those caught up in the excitement; my dissertation is entitled "A Quantitative Study of Dream Content Using an Objective Indicator of Dreaming," University of Miami, 1962.

    For the early eye movement studies, see W. Dement and E. Wolpert, "The Relationship of Eye Movements, Body Motility, and External Stimuli to Dream Content," *Journal of Experimental Psychology* 55 (1958):543–53; H. Roffwarg, W. Dement, J. N. Muzio, and C. Fisher, "Dream Imagery: Relationship of Rapid Eye Movements of Sleep," *Archives of General Psychiatry* 7 (1962):235.

11. E. Diamond, *The Science of Dreams* (Garden City, N.Y.: Doubleday, 1962), p. 17.

12. Ibid., p. 158.

13. Kamiya, "Effects of Drowsiness"; Foulkes, "Dream Reports from Different Stages of Sleep"; A. Rechtschaffen, P. Verdone, and G. Wheaton, "Reports of Mental Activity During Sleep," *Journal of the Canadian Psychiatric Association* 8 (1963):490–514.

14. D. Foulkes and M. Schmidt, "Temporal Sequence and Unit Composition in Dream Reports from Different Stages of Sleep," *Sleep* 16 (1983):277–80.

15. E. Moskowitz and R. J. Berger, "Rapid Eye Movements and Dream Imagery: Are They Related?" *Nature* 224 (1969):613–14.

16. L. D. Jacobs, M. Feldman, and M. B. Bender, "The Patterns of Eye Movements During Sleep," *Transactions of the American Neurological Association* 95 (1970):114–19; L. D. Jacobs, M. Feldman, and M. B. Bender "Eye Movements During Sleep," *Archives of Neurology* 25 (1971):151–59.

17. See Hall, "Caveat Lector!" for a summary of the various kinds of evidence against the "scanning hypothesis." For summaries of the animal evidence, see F. Snyder, "Sleep and Dreaming: Progress in the New Biology of Dreaming," *Association Journal of Psychiatry* 122 (1965):377–91; Crick and Mitchison, "Function of Dream Sleep," p. 112.

18. D. Foulkes and G. Vogel, "Mental Activity and Sleep Onset," *Journal of Abnormal Psychology* 70 (1965):231–43; T. Pivak and D.

Foulkes, "NREM Mentation: Relation to Personality, Orientation Time, and Time of Night," *Journal of Consulting and Clinical Psychology* 32 (1968):144–51; J. Brown and R. D. Cartwright, "Locating NREM Dreaming Through Instrumental Responses," *Psychophysiology* 15 (1978):35–39.

19. C. S. Hall, unpublished quantitative content analysis of REM and NREM reports, provided by David Foulkes, University of California, Santa Cruz, 1969.

20. Foulkes and Schmidt, "Temporal Sequence"; J. S. Antrobus, "REM and NREM Sleep Reports: Comparisons of Word Frequencies by Cognitive Classes," *Psychophysiology* 20 (1983):562–68.

21. A. Kales, F. Hoedemaker, and E. Lichtenstein, "Dream Deprivation: An Experimental Reappraisal," *Nature* 204 (1964): 1337–38; H. Sampson, "Deprivation of Dreaming Sleep by Two Methods," *Archives of General Psychiatry* 13 (1965):79–86; R. D. Cartwright and L. Monroe, "The Relation of Dreaming and REM Sleep: The Effects of REM Deprivation," *Archives of General Psychiatry* 16 (1967):227–80.

22. H. W. Agnew, W. B. Webb, and R. L. Williams, "The Effect of Stage Four Sleep Deprivation," *Electroencephalography and Clinical Neurophysiology* 18 (1965):131–39; W. B. Webb, *Sleep: An Experimental Approach* (New York: Macmillan, 1968).

23. Cartwright, *Night Life;* Snyder, "Sleep and Dreaming"; B. Domhoff and J. Kamiya, "Problems in Dream Content Study with Objective Indicators I. A Comparison of Home and Laboratory Dreams," *Archives of General Psychiatry* 11 (1964):519–24; B. Domhoff and J. Kamiya. "Problems in Dream Content Study with Objective Indicators III. Changes in Dream Content Throughout the Night," *Archives of General Psychiatry* 11 (1964):529–32; C. S. Hall and R. L. Van de Castle, "Studies of Dreams Reported in the Laboratory and at Home," Institute of Dream Research, Monograph Series, no. 1 (1966); B. Domhoff, "Home Dreams and Laboratory Dreams: Home Dreams Are Better," in *Dream Psychology and the New Biology of Dreaming,* ed. M. Kramer (Springfield, Ill.: Charles C. Thomas, 1969); D. Foulkes, "Home and Laboratory Dreams: Four Empirical Studies and a Conceptual Reevaluation," *Sleep* 2 (1979):233–51.

24. D. Foulkes, *Children's Dreams* (New York: John Wiley, 1982).

25. C. A. Meier, H. Ruf, A. Zeigler, P. Schellenberg, and C. S. Hall, "Forgetting of Dreams in the Laboratory," *Perceptual and Motor Skills* 26 (1968):551–57; J. Trinder and M. Kramer, "Dream Recall," *American Journal of Psychiatry* 128 (1971):296–301.

26. C. S. Hall and B. Domhoff, "A Ubiquitous Sex Difference in Dreams," *Journal of Abnormal and Social Psychology* 66 (1963):278–80; C. S. Hall and B. Domhoff, "Aggression in Dreams," *International Journal of Social Psychiatry* 9 (1963):259–67; C. S. Hall and B. Domhoff, "Friendliness in Dreams," *Journal of Social Psychology* 62 (1964):309–14; C. S. Hall, "A Ubiquitous Sex Difference in Dreams Revisited," *Journal of Personality and Social Psychology* 46 (1984): 1109–17.

27. R. L. Van de Castle, *The Psychology of Dreaming* (New York: General Learning Corporation, 1971), p. 37.

28. C. S. Hall, G. W. Domhoff, K. A. Blick, and K. E. Weesner, "The Dreams of College Men and Women in 1950 and 1980: A Comparison of Dream Contents and Sex Differences," *Sleep* 5 (1982):188–94.

29. C. S. Hall and V. J. Nordby, *The Individual and His Dreams* (New York: New American Library, 1972), pp. 19–22, 86–87; R. L. Van de Castle, "Animal Figures in Fantasy and Dreams," in *New Perspectives on Our Lives with Companion Animals,* ed. A. H. Katcher and A. M. Beck (Philadelphia: University of Pennsylvania Press, 1983).

30. Hall and Nordby, *Individual and His Dreams,* pp. 82–83.

31. Ibid.; M. E. Smith and C. S. Hall, "An Investigation of Regression in a Long Dream Series," *Journal of Gerontology* 19 (1964):66–71.

32. C. S. Hall, "Ethnic Similarities in Manifest Dream Contents: A Modest Confirmation of the Theory of Universal Man," Institute of Dream Research (1967); Hall and Nordby, *Individual and His Dreams,* ch. 2. For evidence of other cross-cultural similarities in dream content, see R. M. Griffith, M. Miyagi, and A. Tago, "The Universality of Typical Dreams: Japanese Versus American," *American Anthropologist* 60 (1958):1173–79.

33. Hall and Nordby, *Individual and His Dreams,* pp. 108–9; for full details, see C. S. Hall and R. Lind, *Dreaming, Life, and Literature:*

A Study of Franz Kafka (Chapel Hill: University of North Carolina Press, 1970).

34. Brod, quoted in Hall and Nordby, *Individual and His Dreams,* p. 109.

35. Ibid.

36. The study reveals nothing about Kafka's creativity as a writer. As with the psychoanalytic method, the sources of creativity are not revealed by quantitative content analysis. What Freud wrote in the early thirties in the introduction to a colleague's study of Edgar Allan Poe also applies to this study of Kafka: "Investigations of this kind are not intended to explain an author's genius, but they show what motive forces aroused it and what material was offered to him by destiny." Freud then notes that "there is a particular fascination in studying the laws of the human mind as exemplified in outstanding individuals"; S. Freud, Preface to Marie Bonaparte, *The Life and Works of Edgar Allan Poe, The Standard Edition of the Complete Psychological Works of Sigmund Freud* (London: Hogarth Press, 1964), 22:254.

37. C. S. Hall and B. Domhoff, "The Dreams of Freud and Jung," *Psychology Today,* June 1968, pp. 42–45, 64–65.

38. C. G. Jung, *Memories, Dreams, Reflections* (New York: Pantheon Books, 1961), quoted in Hall and Domhoff, "Dreams of Freud and Jung," p. 44.

39. E. Jones, *The Life and Work of Sigmund Freud,* 3 vols. (New York: Basic Books, 1955), 2:420–21.

40. Freud, *Interpretation of Dreams.*

41. Jung, *Memories, Dreams, Reflections;* C. G. Jung, *Dreams* (Princeton: Princeton University Press, 1974).

42. M. Boss, *The Analysis of Dreams* (New York: Philosophical Library, 1958); M. Boss, *"I Dreamt Last Night . . ."* (New York: Gardner Press, 1977).

43. J. Downing and R. Marmorstein, *Dreams and Nightmares: A Book of Gestalt Therapy Sessions* (New York: Harper & Row, 1973).

44. E. Fromm, *The Forgotten Language* (New York: Grove Press, 1951).

45. N. Fodor, *New Approaches to Dream Interpretation* (New York: Citadel Press, 1962); A. Garma, *The Psychoanalysis of Dreams* (New

York: Quadrangle Books, 1966); T. French and E. Fromm, *Dream Interpretation* (New York: Basic Books, 1964).

46. For recent representatives of this viewpoint, see Crick and Mitchison, "Function of Dream Sleep"; and Evans, *Landscape of the Night.*

47. C. S. Hall, "A Cognitive Theory of Dream Symbols," *Journal of General Psychology* 48 (1953):169–86; C. S. Hall, "A Cognitive Theory of Dreams," *Journal of General Psychology* 49 (1953):273–82; C. S. Hall, *The Meaning of Dreams* (New York: Harper & Row, 1953).

48. Hall and Nordby, *Individual and His Dreams,* p. 146.

49. A. Arkin, *Sleep-Talking: Psychology and Physiology* (Hillsdale, N.J.: Erlbaum, 1981).

50. C. B. Brenneis, "Differences in Male and Female Ego Styles in Manifest Dream Content," unpublished Ph.D. dissertation, University of Michigan, 1967; Hall and Nordby, *Individual and His Dreams,* pp. 14, 194.

51. E. Aronson, "Research in Social Psychology as a Leap of Faith," in *Readings About The Social Animal,* 4th ed., ed. E. Aronson (New York: W. H. Freeman, 1984). In calling for a social psychology that gets new ideas into the field, Aronson writes: "Since I believe that science is a self-correcting enterprise, I would prefer to be provocative than right. Of course, it goes without saying that I do not attempt to be wrong or sloppy. I attempt to do the best I can at the moment and share that less than perfect product with you—my colleagues and critics" (p.6).

Index

Compositor: Innovative Media
Text: 10/12 Bembo
Printer: Thomson-Shore
Binder: John H. Dekker & Sons